CONTENTS

KU-655-799

CONTENTS

INTRODUCTION

I've always thought that people who write books like this are driven by their egos. It's as if the book is designed to convince themselves as much as their readers that the subject matter is an exceptional human being and a cut above everyone else.

Now, here I am writing a book about Jimmy Spithill!

Am I guilty as charged? I hope not.

I hold a deep-seated desire to inspire people who are in tough situations in life, as I can relate to them through my own experiences.

The fact is that I am not a very talented person; I have had to work harder than any sailor I know to get all the way from the very bottom to winning sailing's ultimate prize: the America's Cup. Therefore, my reason for writing this book will have been achieved if just one person who is having a hard time can say after reading it, 'If Jimmy Spithill can accomplish what he has by being true to himself and putting in the hours, then so can I.'

I also hope that by sharing my wide-ranging experiences via these pages I will be contributing something of significance to sailing – a clean and healthy pastime that, like few others, can be enjoyed in many forms the world over by people aged from 8 to 88.

On a personal note, writing this book has certainly taken me out of my comfort zone; it's been a bit of a selfish project. But the fact of the matter is, it's another challenge – and I love challenges.

The Greatest of Comebacks...

The America's Cup is the world's oldest regularly contested sporting trophy, predating the modern Olympic Games by 45 years and the first international competitions for tennis, rugby, soccer, golf and cricket. First contested on the waters off England's Isle of Wight in 1851, it has been a centrepiece for excitement, controversy, misfortune, high drama and groundbreaking technology ever since.

At that notable first competition, a fleet of England's finest sailing vessels raced against a sole American challenger for what was then recognised as the £100 Cup. It was convincingly won by the New York Yacht Club's contender, the schooner *America*, which claimed the trophy by an astonishing margin. In fact, the lead was so great that when Queen Victoria – who was watching from the deck of the Royal Yacht, at anchor off Cowes – asked her attendant which yacht was second, there came the now legendary reply: 'Your Majesty, there is no second.' The first of the British yachts was so far behind the American one that it could not be seen.

Members of the recently formed New York Yacht Club (NYYC) were extremely proud of this achievement, so much so that they soon agreed that the trophy would be renamed in honour of the winning vessel. Thus it became the America's Cup, and subsequently the symbol of international yachting supremacy.

In the years following the first America's Cup match in 1870, the NYYC successfully defended the trophy on no less than 24 occasions – the longest winning streak in international sport. It came to an end after 132 years when, in 1983, the radically designed *Australia II* won the Cup 4–3 in a best-of-seven series off Newport, Rhode Island.

In more recent times, the America's Cup has been blasted to the forefront of sailing dynamics. The cumbersome keelboats that raced for the 'Auld Mug' have now been replaced by the most technologically advanced high-speed catamarans – twin-hulled craft that are so sleek, both aerodynamically and hydrodynamically, that they literally fly across the water at speeds of up to 50 knots!

In conjunction with this spectacular transition from keelboats to cats, one sailor's name has stood above all: Jimmy Spithill.

The event that catapulted Jimmy into the limelight occurred in 2013, when he piloted the American defender, *Oracle Team USA*, to what was arguably the greatest comeback in the history of international sports. From being 8–1 down in a first-to-nine series, Spithill and his team – through tenacity, skill and a liberal dose of spirit – clawed their way back race by race to defeat the New Zealand challenger 9–8 and retain the America's Cup for America.

How Jimmy Spithill rose above his own physical challenges and humble beginnings in Sydney, Australia, and went on to make headlines worldwide makes for inspirational reading.

This is Jimmy Spithill's remarkable story…

Rob Mundle, 2017

ONE

'It Is Unlikely He Will Ever Be Any Good at Sports...'

I was 12 years old and sitting restlessly with a doctor in his consulting room in Sydney, a doctor whom I had already decided I disliked. For a start, he was ignoring me and speaking directly to my obviously anxious mother but, worse still, he had just made a statement that made me mad.

'I'm sure the surgery will solve the problem, but it is unlikely he will ever be any good at sports.'

Instead of reacting, I had to bite my tongue. I needed him to like me because my parents were on the verge of deciding that he should operate on me. That meant he would soon be carving into my right leg with scalpels, drills and any number of other pieces of medical equipment in the hope he could rectify a problem that had been with me since birth. I had had enough … I was getting restless and agitated. All I wanted to do was get the hell out of that stuffy room and go sailing on the bay in front of our house.

What irked me most was that this doctor obviously didn't know my life was already all about being good at sport, despite my right leg being 5cm (2in) shorter than my left, and my right foot being three sizes smaller than the other. That same foot is minus one toe and has two others webbed.

Surprisingly, this physical shortcoming hadn't been a problem until this point in my life, when I had just started high school. Now, it had become a pain in the arse, or more specifically, the lower back, and it was only going to get worse. There was also an emotional element attached to it: I was becoming entertainment for bullies at school – a young, red-headed and freckle-faced kid who also limped was a prime target for their verbal and physical abuse. This bullying was a bit tough for me to cope with then, but in the long run I think it made me a better person, giving me a thicker skin and greater determination to succeed.

As a really young child I remember believing it was normal to only have four toes on your right foot, and that two of the toes should be grown together. But that all changed when I was about four or five years old – the time when I looked at my dad's right foot and thought it was really weird. It had five toes! I laughed and started mocking him: 'Hey Dad, what's wrong with your right foot?' Somewhat surprised, he then told me that feet tend to be of the same size and both have five toes. I was dumbstruck. I didn't speak for 10 minutes; I just sat there and looked at my feet, then looked at his again. Honest to God – before that day I hadn't noticed it. It hadn't occurred to me that for the vast majority of people, their two feet mirror each other.

Regardless, I still didn't consider my right foot to be a problem, even though there were frustrations associated with it. Being three sizes smaller, the shoe I wore on that foot was obviously way too big, and I was too young to realise that there was a simple answer: buy another smaller pair of shoes so I had a right shoe to fit that foot. Nor did I comprehend that the reason my parents hadn't come up with that solution was because it was too expensive for them to buy me two pairs of leather shoes. They were battling financially, so all they could afford was a thick leather platform that attached to the sole and heel of my right shoe so that my limp was minimised.

I came up with my own cost-free way to get round the problem: stuffing socks, rags or whatever into the shoe to wedge my foot into it. However, that didn't work. Too often that shoe just slipped off my foot as I walked down the street, so I had to stop and start the whole procedure again. It wasn't until some years later, when I started playing rugby union at a junior level, that the two-size-shoe approach was finally adopted, because my right boot kept flying off my foot every time I sprinted down the field. My parents must have been as embarrassed as I was by this because thereafter they found the money to buy me two pairs of different-size boots as well as two pairs of regular street shoes.

This was all very well, but it didn't fix my limp. The only way to correct that was through surgery, which was why I found myself in the presence of the doctor I didn't like.

After completing his analysis of my problem, the doctor said to my mother in a reassuring manner that he fully expected the surgery to be successful ... before adding the crushing rider about me probably never being any good at sport. That's when my mind went into a blur. The fact that he was using a chart of the human body mounted on his surgery wall to indicate to my mother the finer details of the operation was of no interest to me. Instead, I was devising ways to prove the doctor wrong when it came to sport. I was thinking about racing my little Manly Junior sailboat, and being able to run faster and tackle harder in a rugby match, all because I had two legs of the same length. That's how I'd prove him wrong.

At the same time my mum was listening intently to what the doctor was saying: 'We are going to stop his left leg growing by removing a growth plate from that leg. That will allow his right leg to catch up then stop growing naturally.'

Needless to say, mum was pretty worried about the operation because she knew the procedure was not without risks. This was groundbreaking surgery – one of the first times it had been attempted anywhere, and the first time the doctor had performed the procedure.

Thankfully it all went well, and after eight weeks on crutches I was able to discard them. A few months later, when I turned 13, I was back to being fully mobile, but it was another two years before both legs were the same length, and limping became a somewhat distant memory. Now, even though my feet remain different, I can run at full pace – in shoes of different sizes!

What the doctor doesn't know is that he changed my life in two ways – through successfully performing the surgery and, more importantly, by suggesting that this boy with a limp would probably never be any good at sport.

I thought of him at the end of my final year of high school in Sydney as I walked up on stage to collect the Pittwater High School

Sportsman of the Year award, presented to me as a result of my successes in sailing, rugby, boxing, Australian rules football, rugby league and cricket.

Thankfully that doctor lit a fire within me, and since then I have done everything possible to be the best in my every endeavour, and let the results do the talking.

'I Am Going to Sail in the America's Cup'

Apparently the first word I ever uttered was not 'Mum' or 'Dad', but 'aats'. My mother told me that every time we drove past the boats docked in Rushcutters Bay, on Sydney Harbour, I'd be looking at them and saying 'aats' over and over.

At the time we were living in a small house in the eastern suburbs, not far from the centre of Sydney. My dad, Arthur, was working as an engineer for a telecommunications company while my mum, Jenny, was employed by Australia's international airline, Qantas, in its city headquarters.

As our family life evolved, my parents experienced a premature mid-life crisis. They were tired of the hustle and bustle of the urban environment; it was time to depart the concrete jungle and embrace a way of living that valued nature more than neighbours.

After some consideration they decided they wanted to live on the banks of the Hawkesbury River, a spectacular waterway that meanders 120 kilometres (75 miles) inland from Broken Bay and Pittwater, just 30 kilometres (19 miles) up the coast from Sydney Harbour. In little time they found their dream property and, soon after, a price was agreed with the seller. They paid the deposit and contracts were drawn up … but while that was happening they were gazumped. Someone had come in, offered more money and secured the deal!

My parents were shattered, but from where I stand I can look back and say I'm really glad it happened. If they had bought that property I'd probably be riding horses today and not be sailing 'aats' or, more specifically, the world's fastest sailboats.

Not long afterwards, fate dealt another good hand, one that really set my life on its course. Mum and Dad had a 35ft sailboat that we cruised from Sydney Harbour up to Pittwater and surrounding waterways on a regular basis. I was not yet two when, on one of these excursions, we anchored off Elvina Bay – a scenic, secluded and tree-lined inlet in the south-west corner of beautiful Pittwater – to meet up with a family friend, nicknamed 'The Rock', who lived on nearby Scotland Island.

Mum and Dad enjoyed that well-protected anchorage so much that we went back there almost every time we cruised on Pittwater. Then came the day when 'The Rock' told my parents that there was a tiny shack in Elvina Bay for sale. It was nothing special – a very basic little one-bedroom hut built from the cheapest building material of the day – sheets of fibro – but it was perched atop a little hill on an acre of land where the front boundary was the bay and the rear one a beautiful and very bushy national park.

Mum and Dad immediately fell in love with the place and its potential, even though it was in the worst condition of all the 20 houses located in the bay. It was on a peninsula, offered expansive water views and was only accessible by boat. For them, it was as good as living on an island. It even had a tiny boatshed and jetty on the waterfront. The worst thing about it was the price: it was at the limit of their slim wallet. However, instead of giving up, they formulated a plan – buy, renovate and sell – though this was to be a scheme they would never implement. In due course, everything fell into place for them and we became Elvina Bay residents in 1982.

To move to a one-bedroom shack on a hill with no road access and two kids – a three-year-old and a four-month-old – took guts, and my parents obviously had plenty. Later, they would tell me that waking up there that first morning, surrounded by magnificent eucalyptus trees, listening to the raucous cackle of the kookaburras and seeing a spectacular water view, convinced them they had found their nirvana. Most importantly, it was a great place for kids.

Their only worry was that my sister, Katie, and I would be attracted to the water, so they would have to keep an eye on us since we were too young to swim. As it turned out, I stayed out of trouble but Katie fell in twice and had to be rescued, something that was witnessed both times by my grandparents on my father's side while they were visiting from Sydney's landlocked western suburbs. Perhaps not surprisingly, seeing these accidents prompted my grandmother to declare most adamantly: 'Arthur, this happens all the time. It is dangerous. And you are so far away from everything! How can you live here?'

They were also unimpressed by the fact that our humble home was literally falling apart. But none of that worried our parents. We soon learned to swim, and as far as the house was concerned, Dad demonstrated that he was a great builder. He soon had the transformation of the shack underway, but it was no easy task. He had to load everything needed on to our tiny 'tinny' – an aluminium dinghy – at the closest village, Church Point, then transport it across the water to our home. Once there he had to lift it all off the tinny – timber, tiles, stone and cement – and carry it up the stairs to the house.

As a kid in Elvina Bay, you were either on the water or in the bush. Since there were no roads, there were no cars, so Mum and Dad let us loose from a very young age. Yet we weren't completely cut off – one of the great things about Elvina Bay is that it's not too far from the rest of the world; in just 90 minutes we could be in the heart of Sydney's central business district.

It may be a cliché that it takes a village to raise a child, but in a tiny waterfront community such as Elvina Bay, where nobody locked their doors, it really was like that. I was one of the youngest kids among 10 boys and a couple of girls always roaming the area and having fun. It was a bit like a waterfront Wild West for youngsters. You knew everyone, there were no rules, and you could do whatever you wanted as long as you got home in time for dinner. So we'd be off all day sailing, swimming, scampering through the bush or climbing waterfalls. The only time we were really pushing it was when we'd sneak out of the house at night and go barefoot into the bush ... because in the Australian bush, pretty much everything can kill you! I don't know how we got away with it, but somehow we all survived.

Of course there were some downsides and hardships associated with living in the bay, but you tolerated these as part of your chosen lifestyle. You accepted that bush fires could come charging through the vegetation at the back of the bay and threaten your home, and that a huge thunderstorm could roll over the hills in the west and knock out your electricity supply for days – but you prepared for those eventualities and lived with them. For me, one of the most important things was the community spirit and the fact that there was always someone there to help.

The water became an increasingly powerful magnet for me, so the older I got the more time I spent on it and in it. When I was five, I was given a little kid's-size windsurfer, so just about any time the wind was blowing on Elvina Bay and Pittwater you'd find me out there, always sailing as fast as I could.

In the Australian vernacular, my parents were battlers, always trying to make ends meet financially. A small amount of relief came for them when they rented the boatshed to a friend who used it as a weekender. For me, he was a friend with a benefit: he had a 14ft Hobie Cat. It's perhaps fitting that some of my first sailing experiences took place on a catamaran, and now here I am sailing the world's fastest cats.

I loved that Hobie. Before I had sufficient skills to take it out myself, I'd wait impatiently for Dad to come home from work so we could go sailing. Then, on weekends, the kids from around the bay would pile on to the catamaran and off we'd go on an adventure. Quite often there would be 10 of us on the thing, swimming around it, diving off it and sailing around the bay. I could not have wanted a better life.

School days were all about trying not to miss the ferry that took us to Church Point. Each morning, as the little blue-and-white boat chugged around the headland and into the bay, the skipper would blow the horn, a signal to me that I had one minute to finish whatever I was doing, run down the fire trail and leap aboard. If you missed the boat, you were in serious trouble with both the teachers and your parents.

For some reason, I always seemed to be the last kid to jump aboard, just as the boat was leaving the jetty. I remember one morning when, with my heart pounding after my sprint to the dock, I landed on the deck feeling a high level of relief.

'Morning, James.'

'Morning, Len.'

'That was a close one, mate. One day you're gonna miss it.'

'No worries Len, didn't even crack a sweat getting here.'

From Elvina Bay it was two stops to Church Point – the gateway to civilisation. Once there, we'd catch the bus to Mona Vale and get to school in plenty of time. Usually…

I distinctly remember one instance when the journey to school didn't go quite as planned. On this particular morning a mate and I were mucking around on our BMX bikes, having so much fun that we were oblivious to the time and missed the ferry. Simply put, we were in deep because there was no other way for us to get to school in time. Then came the flash! We could swim to Church Point! Great idea! We rode our bikes through the bush to the point of land closest to our destination, took off most of our clothes, jumped in the water and started swimming. It was about a mile – a long way for us – but fortunately there were plenty of boat mooring buoys in the bay, so we could stop and take a breather when we needed to (I realise now we gave no thought whatsoever to the possible presence of sharks!). Once we reached shore a local kindly drove us to school where, still wet, we crept unnoticed into the 'lost and found' room and unearthed some school uniforms we could wear. We then snuck into class without being detected and sat at our desks. Mission accomplished! The teacher never knew, and neither did our parents.

I was nine when Katie and I were presented with two things: a little brother, who was named Thomas (Tom for short), and an unexpected opportunity to own our own sailboat. The latter came via a strike of good fortune when our father realised a neighbour was throwing out an old Manly Junior sailing dinghy as part of the annual Elvina Bay junk and rubbish collection. Dad had no hesitation in asking if we could have it, and the neighbour gladly handed it over. It was snub nosed, 8ft 8in (2.6m) long, built from plywood, heavy and in need of repairs … but for us, one man's trash was another man's treasure. We helped Dad fix it up, gave it a coat of blue paint, and named it *Ventura* after a yacht Dad had owned before he had kids.

* * *

From the day we first launched *Ventura*, Katie and I couldn't spend enough time on the water – we were out on the bay at every opportunity, and for much of that time Dad was alongside us in the tinny, forever shouting out instructions about how best to sail the boat.

While we kids of the bay always had fun, there was also a nice level of camaraderie between the 'grown-ups' living there. At least once a week – usually on a Friday evening – almost everyone, including us kids, would get together on the ferry wharf over at Church Point for a few beers. We called it the 'The Church Point Hilton', but trust me, it was nothing like the Hilton. The cross-section of people was amazing – from labourers to magistrates and everyone in between. Beers would be going down like water, and as they did so, the gathering became more animated and the laughter louder. Also, just about everyone from the bay who owned a dog had it there, so dog fights were not unusual. Basically, this was a typical outdoor Aussie drinking session.

One day Dad came home from a session at the 'Hilton' and told us that he had heard there was a Manly Junior race coming up the following Sunday at Avalon Sailing Club, on the other side of Pittwater on the mainland. Although Katie was not overly enthused by sailing at that time, this was awesome news to my ears – it was our first chance ever to race a sailboat.

We were both up early on what was a beautiful morning to rig and launch *Ventura*. The wind was very light, so it took us about an hour to sail across to Avalon, with Dad alongside in the tinny. Once there, we proudly pulled our boat up on to the beach amid a fleet of Manly Juniors, only to realise in an instant that there was a big difference between about 90 per cent of those boats and ours: they were made of fibreglass and had new sails.

Upon our arrival, a lot of the kids from the club came over to our boat and looked at it as if it were something out of a museum. Questions and statements followed:

'Look at that old thing! Are you going to compete in that?'

'It is made of wood, and look at the shitty old sails, ha-ha!'

'Do you really think you can race in such an old thing? It is older than my grandmother!'

Upset by this abuse, Katie started crying, and I was really pissed off. Luckily, however, Dad saw what was going on so he came over and put his arms around us. 'It doesn't matter what people think or say,' he counselled. 'You've been sailing your boat all the time. You built it and repaired it – so now just get out there and see what happens.'

With that said, he explained the course to us and how the starting procedure worked. We pushed *Ventura* back into the water, leapt aboard and headed for the start line. The wind had really strengthened by the time the race got underway, so Katie and I worked hard trimming the sails and using our weight to balance the boat. We were out there for about two hours, and during that period I didn't really have any idea what was happening with the other boats – we were just completing the course as best we could. Finally, when we crossed the finish line, there was a sound we weren't expecting: the firing of the gun to signal we'd won the race ... our very first race!

When we got ashore and dragged *Ventura* up the beach, Dad was almost as excited as we were. Then the same kids gathered around our boat again, but this time they weren't laughing.

From that moment on, neither Katie nor I could get enough of sailing. One race had changed our lives. It was a win that taught me two valuable lessons early in life, and which I still heed to this day: *Let the results do the talking, and never judge a book by its cover.*

A few days later we got a letter from an official of the Avalon Sailing Club.

'Dear James and Katie,

Congratulations on your great win on Sunday! A win in your first race must be like scoring a century in your first Test Cricket Match.

It was a tough race, but every time I saw you, you were well and truly in control. Well done.

The club can expect great things from you in the future.

Yours sincerely,

Ian Craig

Hon. Secretary'

Sailing with Katie also taught me the importance of being a team player. Initially, this wasn't easy – brothers and sisters don't always get along – but it worked for us. However, I must confess that I will never forget the time I shouted something so mean at her while we were racing *Ventura* that she cried. Fortunately, Dad stepped in and told me to go easy on her, that I should respect the team. This caused the penny to drop for me, and I quickly realised that the noisier you are when sailing a boat, the less confident you are.

This has proven to be the case on every boat I've sailed on. On a quiet boat, the crew know what they are doing – they are confidently engaged in their job. Of course, you yell to each other when it is very windy or noisy and communication is essential, but in my opinion, to yell at someone during a sailboat race just because you can simply means that something's wrong in the structure of the crew – and that something might be the skipper. For me, it indicates that respect is not there, and without that you won't win. The good guys always keep it together – especially in tough moments.

* * *

It wasn't long after Katie and I won that race at Avalon Sailing Club that I made a declaration to my parents: 'I am going to sail in the America's Cup!' Dad immediately humoured me, replying, 'Of course you are.'

The statement didn't have any real impact on them – after all, nine-year-olds say silly things all the time – but I already knew, for one very good reason, that that was where I wanted to go with my sailing. Elvina Bay in particular and Pittwater in general was home to an incredible number of professional sailors – Australian sailing legends, many of whom had played important roles in Australian America's Cup challenges. Among them were Iain Murray, Adam Beashel, Colin Beashel, Ken Beashel, Hugh Treharne, Phil Smidmore, Grant Simmer and Rob Brown. In fact, four of the *Australia II* team that won the America's Cup in 1983 lived in or near Elvina Bay.

This sporting victory in 1983 literally stopped Australia in its tracks. The moment when *Australia II* crossed the finish line was the signal for unbridled celebrations Australia-wide; even motorists stopped their cars in the middle of Sydney Harbour Bridge, in rush hour, and danced around them. I was really too young to remember much of it, but so great was the impact that our sports-crazy prime minister at the time, Bob Hawke, went live on national TV that morning, drenched in champagne, and declared: 'Any boss who sacks a worker for not turning up today is a bum.'

Of all the locals, Rob Brown became my mentor. Outside the America's Cup arena he was a champion in the amazing 18ft skiffs. The first extreme sailboats to appear on TV on a regular basis, these skiffs were light, fast, grossly over-powered boats that were way ahead of their time. Their racing became my favourite TV entertainment – every time the 18s were on, I'd be glued to the box, along with a huge number of other followers, watching sailboat racing as it had never been done before. Rob was among the best, and whenever I saw him I could not talk enough about sailing, the skiffs and the America's Cup.

As far as I was concerned, my rationale was simple – here was a bunch of local guys who were, or had been, professional sailors. I already loved sailing, so why not be paid to do it? Still, mum and dad couldn't see how a kid my age could already know his career path in life. They let it be, but I didn't.

They were, however, impressed by the fact that I'd become an entrepreneur at the age of 10. Some people had weekenders in the bay – small cottages to which they'd go to escape suburbia for a few days. Many of them had small boats on moorings or at their jetties, and quite often, when it rained a lot, the boats would start filling with water. 'James Spithill Enterprises' provided a pump-out service for these boats so they didn't sink. However, there was a much greater benefit in this business for me than just earning a bit of pocket money: if you're a kid living in the suburbs you dream of your first motorbike or car, but if you're a kid living where I did, you dream of small powerboats with big outboard motors. Imagine my delight, then, when a number of my customers allowed me to use their boats while they were away.

My next problem was school. I just felt that it was getting in the way of sailing. It was also an obstacle to having fun with my mates and, on a more personal note, exposed me to bullying. As already mentioned, my red hair and freckles made me a target for a handful of older kids. As a result, my friends and I ended up in a few scraps. It also taught me the truth of the saying about redheads: if you have red hair you are good at two things – running, for obvious reasons, and fighting, because after a while you just get sick of running.

In fact, it was the bullying that ultimately drove me to do well at sport in school. In the last year of primary school there was a try-out for the rugby team, and in order to make the grade you had to play against the current team and tackle them. Essentially they had the ball, so you were tackling all the time. This suited me fine. I had no problem tackling big guys – I'd been doing it all the time at home in the bay where most of the kids were older or bigger and we would play in the dirt. What really excited me about the try-out was that the majority of the guys on the opposing team, those with the ball, were the bullies … so I just went for it, with one goal: to hurt these guys as much as I could. Once on the field, the suppressed anger caused by all those beatings my mates and I had copped could be unleashed without fear of retribution. By the end of the match I had a fair bit of blood over me, but Mr Brown, the coach, was pretty impressed: 'Mate, you are picked. You are on the team. I have never seen such disregard for one's own well-being. That's some of the best tackling I've seen – now head off to the sick bay and get that blood cleaned up.'

My actions silenced some of the bullies, and for me it confirmed that, in sport, it didn't matter where you are from or what you look like – it comes down to who works the hardest and who wants it.

Moreover, the incident made me understand something else: there was definitely more room for sport than academia in my life! So, apart from getting a chance to shine on the rugby pitch – where the bullies and I eventually became good mates – I played pretty much anything else I could at school.

Looking back at my school days, I realise that the most boring part was sitting on the ferry on the way home. It was unbelievably boring, mainly because Elvina Bay was the last stop; the little ferry would leave Church Point and amble across to Scotland Island and around all the other bays before getting to our dock. So, to liven up the monotonous journey, we, the kids from Elvina Bay, created our own fun – the thruster. As we approached our stop, we'd take off our shoes and as soon as we had leapt off the ferry and on to the dock we'd drop our school bags and shoes on the jetty and jump into the water behind the ferry as it departed so we were tossed around by the swirling prop wash. Obviously we didn't think about what might happen if the ferry driver put it into reverse instead of forward!

This was all part of a great lifestyle we enjoyed in the bay. We never had any fears. It was safe and we were 'waterproof', and that caused less stress for our parents. We even banded together and built our own BMX bike track with jumps as big as we dared. Yes, there was the occasional accident, like a broken arm or shoulder, but we just considered it collateral damage that often came when you were having a good time. Snakes were always a problem, but we were fortunate to live near a guy who was an expert when it came to handling them. We saw quite a bit of him, especially when we tried to keep some little rabbits in a hutch outside our house, which resulted in snakes frequently mistaking our property for their snack shop. Cue a phone call to our 'snake man'.

'Hey Mike, we have a snake in our backyard…'

'No worries, I'll come over.'

He'd then come out in a flash and grab the snake by the neck and carry it into the bush, where he'd let it go. I was always amazed watching him, and he knew it. So, one day, not surprisingly given my curiosity, he asked: 'You want to try it? I'll show you how to hold them.' I nodded with some degree of hesitation, feeling excited at the same time.

The chance to give it a go arrived the day a diamond python slithered into our place looking for bunny snacks. This was a snake you just couldn't kill … although non-venomous – they constrict their prey – it was about 1.8m (6ft) long.

'All right, James, you take this one,' Mike said. 'Just walk up into the bush as far as you can, throw it in the bush and come home.'

I was only 11 years old, and as I was carrying this python into the bush it started wrapping itself around me and squeezing my arm. It was trying to kill me! In no time I was getting pins and needles, then I realised I couldn't hold its head because my arm was getting so numb that my grip was becoming weaker. So, using my other hand, which was also holding its head, I tried to peel this freakin' snake off my arm, but it was too strong. There I was, alone in the bush, trying to get rid of the python and too proud to shout

out that I needed help. Instead, I became more determined to get rid of it. My arm was getting more and more numb by the minute, and I felt the fear rise in me, but I still knew I couldn't let it take control. With my free arm I eventually got a bit of leverage under the snake's still-slithering and cool body and, using my elbow for more leverage, I forced the python to ease its grip just a little bit. That was all I needed: I was in control again and able to prise the bugger off. Finally, with both arms free, I was able to lift this very unhappy, hissing and writhing snake above my head and hurl it into the bush, thinking 'never again'. I then walked out of the bush as though nothing had happened and jogged back down to the house where Mike was waiting.

'How'd you go, mate?'

'Yeah, no worries – let me know if you find some more.'

I was clutching my arm when I said that with an air of nonchalance, and I reckon that was enough for Mike to realise that things hadn't exactly gone to plan, but he didn't ask any questions. Instead, I am sure he knew that I had triumphed over my fear and he didn't want to destroy my moment.

Dodging a Bullet

At Mona Vale Public School – the junior school I attended – fights among the kids were a recurring thing. It was boys being boys. If there was going to be a fight, there were three rules: it would be after school, it would take place on the field across the road from the school, and parents and teachers were never to know in advance … which meant we were all sworn to secrecy. However, I'm sure many of the parents did know because there was no other reason for a large number of schoolkids to be streaming across the road from the school and into the field. They must have just ignored it.

I had no interest in being part of these fights, either as a participant or as a spectator, until my final year, when I had no option: one of the more popular kids challenged me and I couldn't step away from it. My opponent was one of the school bullies and a really good surfer. To put it bluntly, I was absolutely shitting myself in the days leading up to the fight because I wasn't a fighter and he was. I was sure he was going to flog the living daylights out of me. How was I going to cope, I asked myself, and how was I going to be able to walk away when it was all over with some degree of pride still in place? The only thing I could do was practise, and the only way to do that was to hang an old rubber boat fender from a tree at home and begin punching it as hard as I could. It wasn't much, but at least I was making an effort.

Before long, I had to accept that the only thing to do was just get the fight done. So, on the designated day I walked out on to the field at the agreed time and stepped into the human ring the other kids had formed. From that moment it was 'on'. For me, it felt like I was in a weird movie – the kids were screaming and shouting as we packed punches into each other. Then it turned into a wrestling match with the two of us rolling around in the dirt. There's no denying I did cop a bit of a hiding, but I still managed to get the odd shot in and earn everyone's respect. For a start, I had turned up to fight the kid everyone expected to win, and I had sunk a couple of good punches into him as well. The fight ended when all the other kids decided they'd seen enough, and at that moment I can remember the feeling of a massive weight being lifted off my shoulders. The other guy was obviously the winner, but even so, I gave a good account of myself in what was my first real contact with boxing. Ironically, my opponent and I ended up being really good mates.

The bonus that arose from this fight was that I was never again worried about copping a hiding. I was also toughened up by playing rugby, since I almost always played against an age group older than my own. This meant I had no option but to throw myself into the action and take any punishment that might come my way. I can also say today that I wasn't proud of being involved in a fight at school, but I could never just stand by and see mates being beaten up or picked on just because they were somehow different. That used to frustrate the hell out of me, and I would step in. Of course, not all the fights were noble, but whatever happened, you always stood up for your friends.

One day in particular early on in high school stands out vividly. My mates and I had copped the worst hiding we'd ever received and, as we walked away from it pretty battered and bruised, we somehow ended up in an industrial area in Mona Vale. As we wandered along the street, we noticed that a boxing gym called The Foundry had just opened.

It so happened that the owner, a typically large and fit-looking Tongan, Gilbert Guttenbiel, was standing outside as we went past. 'Hey, why don't you come in and have a look, boys?'

He didn't have to ask twice. We followed him into a hall with an elevated ring in the middle where a couple of guys were sparring, and boxing punching bags hanging from the ceiling. New as it was, you could already smell sweat and leather, and in between the sound of the punches being exchanged in the ring you could hear a faint hum from the fluorescent lights.

'Why don't you do a training session?' Gilbert asked. All six of us liked that idea, but for me there was something deeper –

I instantly had a feeling in my body that said 'this is what I want'. Soon after, we all started training there a couple of times a week, but as things progressed my friends dropped off one by one. Eventually I was the only person who persisted, but I didn't care – I loved it. During the first month I regularly went home with a black eye or a rearranged lip, damage that led to Mum asking: 'What is going on? Is this boxing such a good idea, really?'

Deep down, though, I think my dad liked what I was doing. I was 15, and one of the smallest guys in a gym that had a nice older-brother mentality. If I was walking along any of the local streets with my new boxing mates, it seemed like I had my own security team – we were family. The brotherhood, the hard training, the focus – I was hooked for life. It all led to many good things, including meeting a guy who is still one of my best mates: Shannon Pilon.

This experience also caused positive things to happen at school: we could finally turn the table on the bullies. From year 10 onwards, we had no more issues with them – it was payback time, and I have to say that at the time revenge never tasted so sweet. I realise today that what we did to the bullies often wasn't right, but it sure solved many problems.

Pittwater High School which I moved to the following year had a subject that I really liked – 'Sports' – and in particular, sailing! I couldn't sign up soon enough.

In those days, sailing wasn't a mainstream sport for schools. In recent times in Australia, however, it has gone from being a peripheral pastime to a vastly popular activity, and I think to a great extent we can thank the last two America's Cup events for that.

Back then, Peter Mulholland, who was our design, technology and woodworking teacher at the school, was also the sailing master. He organised all the sailing training on Pittwater and took us to regattas across our home state and in other parts of Australia. Here, we constantly tried our hardest to defend our colours, even though we were the absolute underdogs. Pittwater High was a public school without money, and we were always up against private schools such as Cranbrook, Knox Grammar and Scots College, which had plenty of cash at their disposal. These schools always seemed to have new boats, whereas Pittwater High had one vintage Pacer-class dinghy that was close to being a collector's item. Fortunately, nearby Royal Prince Alfred Yacht Club often came to our rescue and loaned the school boats. Our budget was so tight that we wore the school's maroon rugby jerseys for sailing regattas at the weekend then had to have them back at the school on Monday morning so they could be washed and readied for us to wear for rugby games on Tuesday. How did we fare sailing against those wealthy schools? Well, more often than not, the kids from Pittwater High beat the rich kids.

The fact that the Pacer dinghy was slow proved to be a bonus for us: it made us think about tactics as well as boat speed. Sailboat racing is a thinking game. It's as much about learning to use the rules to your advantage as it is about boat speed. You can use your boat as a weapon, but you cannot deliberately crash into other boats.

In one-on-one match racing – which is what you see in the America's Cup – you can hunt down your opponent even before the start with the intention of forcing them into a breach of the rules governing the race, of which there are many. For example, if you can shoehorn them into a position where you have right of way and are forced to change course to avoid a collision, the umpires aboard small boats on the course can signal a penalty turn for your rival, which means you have an immediate advantage by going into the lead unchallenged.

Apart from having good boat speed, the key to success in all racing – but in match racing in particular – is to keep your cool and be able to make the right decisions quickly. In a monohull match race the outcome is usually dependent on which boat is best placed at the start. If you can outmanoeuvre your opponent then chances are you can cover their every move all the way to the finish and claim victory. In today's America's Cup, however, the super-fast catamarans – which are capable of 30 knots (55km/h or 34mph) upwind and 50 knots (93km/h or 58mph) downwind – have brought an exciting new dimension to sailing – one that makes it a true spectator sport. Yes, the start is still important, but because the sailing is so fast, unforgiving and intense, the excitement and uncertainty remain until the first boat crosses the finishing line. .

From a young age, when I first got into match racing in small keelboats, my goal was always to try to sail as aggressively as possible with the intention of gaining three penalties over my opponent. This meant the opposing crew would be 'black flagged' by the umpires and consequently disqualified from the race. This gives you a great psychological advantage over all other opponents. In short, the rules are the rules, and I use them. It's all part of the game ... winning is winning.

Even so, I did have one interesting experience in a match-racing series in New Zealand when I was just 15 years old. In this particular race, we had two penalties over our opponent in pretty quick succession, and soon after we forced him into another mistake. This meant he should have been disqualified, but the umpires refused to acknowledge it with a black flag! I was amazed, so much so that at the end of the day I approached one of the umpires. 'Why didn't you give him a third penalty?' I asked. The official replied: 'Something like this has never happened before. We felt that what you were doing was a breach of sportsmanship.'

I bit my tongue and walked away, thinking: 'That's complete bullshit.' Why would it be a breach of sportsmanship, just because I was sailing at the top of my ability and pushing my opponent to the limit while staying within the rules? You win or you lose – it's as simple as that. It was fair play, not bad sportsmanship! That ruling – or lack of it – only made me try harder in the future, and this resulted in me being super-aggressive in the America's Cup. It was as much a psychological ploy as a tactical manoeuvre; I wanted to embarrass my opponents by out-sailing them ... I wanted to force them into a bad start, cause them to make bad decisions and make them play catch-up. I'd do whatever would help gain the team an advantage.

In our school races, each team comprised three sailing dinghies, and it was the combined total of the points scored by each boat in a team that decided the result. Our little public school might have lacked funding, but we had plenty of talented sailors, including my sister, Katie, who skippered one of our team boats. Over the years we made sure we went to the events that really mattered: our state championship (the New South Wales Championship) and the Australian championship. We also competed in some international events in Australia and New Zealand.

When I was not sailing for the school on the weekends I was either sailing in the Royal Prince Alfred Yacht Club's youth development programme or competing in regattas. This was a fantastic opportunity for a kid like me who couldn't afford his own boat. For around 100 bucks you got coaching, entry fees to competitions, and could sail as much as you wanted – these were exciting times for youngsters.

Katie and I had a regatta pretty much every weekend, so the whole family would get up at the crack of dawn, take the tinny to the mainland, then Dad would drive us to the venue. While Katie and I were out on the water, Mum and Dad would find a spot close to the course where they could follow us through the binoculars. It was wonderful support for us. Even when we had a bad day, Dad would always find something positive to say, such as: 'Geez, you really picked that wind shift well on the second beat. That spinnaker leg was really fast.'

By contrast, we saw some other parents berate and shout at their kids if they performed poorly, but our mum and dad never did. Often the consequence for the hostile parents was that their kids were soon turned off the sport.

Just about every time we returned home from one of these regattas there was a party happening at the 'Church Point Hilton' or someone's house in the bay. With it being such a tight-knit community it was always 'open house' – everyone was invited. They were great times: kids were running around everywhere laughing and having fun, while the parents brought all the food, beer and wine. There was only one rule – there were no rules ... except 'have a good time'.

This was a period when there was a significant drinking culture in Australia, and there was always a lot going on at these parties. As the grown-ups became more 'lubricated', so the stories among them got better and better. Needless to say there were some unfortunate incidents, none worse than the time one of Dad's best mates was killed while heading home from a session at 'Church Point Hilton'. It was dark and he apparently didn't see a large powerboat coming towards him. The two boats collided and he died as a result of the impact.

On another night, it was Dad who was almost killed. He was coming home from Church Point and was halfway across the bay when the small outboard motor stopped because the fuel line had detached itself. What he didn't realise in his wrecked state was that the motor was in gear and on full throttle, so when he put the fuel line back on and started the boat, it took off faster than a dog chasing a car. Not surprisingly, Dad went straight over the back and into the tide. Luckily the outboard was at full lock so the boat kept going around in tight circles and, even more fortunately, the fuel line somehow detached itself from the motor and the boat stopped. Dad was then able to swim over to it, clamber aboard and head home.

Initially I thought of this episode as being one of my father's occasional misadventures, but I slowly came to realise that wherever Dad was at night, there was always drinking going on. He was not a raging fall-over binge drinker, he was more of an enthusiastic 'stay topped up' social drinker. This wasn't unusual for many of the residents who were regulars at the 'Church Point Hilton' – no one raised an eyebrow if you rewarded yourself with a beer or 10 at the end of a hard day's work. But when alcohol is not a reward any more, when it starts having a medicinal value for you, then you are in trouble, and by the early 1990s my dad had crossed that line. He'd become an alcoholic, a problem that was cultivated within our living environment and our family – we were surrounded by heavy drinkers.

My dad is one of the best blokes I know, a 'mate' who bailed me out of trouble several times. But when he was drunk he was annoying, loud, unreasonable and, on more than one occasion, simply embarrassing. Fortunately he was able to hold on to his job, but he lost his licence for driving under the influence ... three times! What surprised me most was the way the matter was dealt with in court; the length of the suspension was minimal because he needed his licence for work, but at no stage was anything ever suggested that could help him deal with his problem with alcohol. All I can say is thank God he never had any accidents while driving.

In my opinion, when it comes to alcohol today there is a big cultural difference between Australia and Mediterranean countries such as Italy and Spain. In some parts of Europe, kids often enjoy a glass of wine at dinner with their family in a pleasant atmosphere at home. But for a lot of Australians it's still all about getting drunk at a young age, often as a consequence of peer pressure from mates.

I was 15 when I finally got the chance. I went to a party at Newport, on the other side of Pittwater, with an older mate with whom I sailed quite a lot. From the moment we arrived I wanted to be 'one of the boys'. I felt obliged to keep downing the beers at the same rate as my friends, who'd had plenty of practice ... and there was a girl at the party who I wanted to impress. I lasted just a few rounds with the guys – then I threw up for the rest of the night! I made a complete fool of myself, so much so that the girl showed no interest in me whatsoever.

As I progressed through my teenage years it seemed there was a party almost every weekend, and I did my best to be there. However, I differed greatly from my mates in one critical respect: I would always finish my training – be it sailing or boxing – before I joined any party, day or night.

I got into serious training when I was 16. Every Sunday morning I did strength-training sessions under the guidance of a coach, Mick Miller, at the yacht club. These started at 7am, and if you weren't on time you weren't punished – your mates were! They had to do a big number of extra push-ups while you watched. It was agony for me to be subjected to this the first time I arrived late, and the punishment worked: I was never late again. I think there was also a psychological advantage associated with these early-morning training sessions ... it was good to think you were out of bed and making an inspired effort while your opponents were still asleep. It's a theory confirmed by the fact that the three of us who were most committed to this programme all went on to become world sailing champions.

Unfortunately, Dad's alcohol intake didn't slow down: he simply refused to accept he had a problem. I think it takes personal insight or an emotional jolt from the outside for most alcoholics to realise they are in trouble. In my dad's case, this shock came when, in 1994, Mum declared she had had enough of his drinking, packed up what important possessions she could carry, put Katie, Tom and me aboard a boat, left Elvina Bay and headed for an apartment she'd rented in nearby Mona Vale.

Finally, here was a serious wake-up call for Dad – it was the shock he needed for his own benefit, and ours. In a very short time he was on the phone to Mum: 'Do you want to come back and we can give it another go, Jenny?' To which she replied: 'No, Arthur, I am not coming back to Elvina Bay. If you want another go, we'll do it on the mainland [which was anywhere beyond Church Point].'

Dad stuck it out for a while, but eventually he gave in. We sold the house in Elvina Bay and he came and lived with us in a house up the road from the yacht club. The location was perfect for me, but I really did miss Elvina Bay and the lifestyle. Now, though, I could walk to the Royal Prince Alfred Yacht Club and ride my bike to school in a few minutes. Equally important was the fact that just over the hill to the east was the ocean and beautiful Northern Beaches where we could go surfing.

Dad tried to sober up, he really did. He attended Alcoholics Anonymous and sought whatever other guidance he could, but having two yacht clubs and the legendary Northern Beaches pub, The Newport Arms, nearby initially proved too much of a temptation for him. In the end – and luckily before Mum's patience ran out – he realised he didn't want to lose us. I'd say this revelation was the direct result of the AA meetings, where he could see the destruction that alcohol had caused in other people's lives, decent people just like him.

It took him three years and three trips to a clinic to complete his 12 steps and come dry, and I'm proud to say that since 1996 Dad has been sober; he hasn't touched a drop. To witness this turnaround and his ability to change for the better has been one of the most inspiring things, if not the most inspiring thing, in my life. Had he not given up the drink my career would not have been the same, and I may not have followed the path I'm on.

I also have to say, full credit to Mum: her moving out no doubt saved the family.

Like all teenage boys, I did manage to get myself into trouble at times, but it was mostly what I saw as harmless fun. For instance, I'd take the tinny and tilt the outboard motor so that it ran at full clip with the bow high in the air and the stern barely in the water. This made it the perfect wave jumper – you'd be out on Pittwater at the weekends waiting for big powerboats to come charging along, dragging a huge wake behind them. I'd head for the waves at full speed, just to see how much 'air' I could achieve.

Wake jumping was fantastic fun ... until ... OK, I'll confess here ... on more than one occasion I flipped the boat upside down and 'drowned' the motor, by which I mean it detached itself from the boat and sank. Fortunately I had the good sense to take a bearing from features on the land, so I had an accurate fix on where I had lost the motor. One of my best mates, Matt Blackwood, who was with me in his own boat, could then come over and pick me up out of the water each time it happened (I would also return the favour sometimes), and I then had to go home and sheepishly explain to my father what I'd done. The good news was that one of Dad's mates was a diver with the local water police, and he was happy to help recover the motor because he could treat it as an exercise. Another positive was that my bearings proved remarkably accurate – each time Dad's mate did the dive he found the motor within a few metres of the spot. Still, that didn't make me feel too excited since my parents had to foot the bill for the repairs.

Another event that was much harder to laugh off and far more stupid than flipping the dinghy occurred when I was 16 years old, when we'd just finished a round of the youth development programme at Royal Prince Alfred Yacht Club. It had been a very successful year – we'd won pretty much everything there was to win. At the awards night at the yacht club we were enjoying a large and well-deserved celebration at which my mates were plying me with beers. Afterwards, five of us were heading off to an after-party in a borrowed small Suzuki jeep – the type you see being rented in Hawaii and elsewhere as fun cars for holidaymakers – no roof, two seats in the front, a bench seat in the back and a roll bar over the top.

'I'm too drunk. Can anybody drive?' were the words used by my mate, who was waving the car keys in the air while we all laughed at him. 'Yep, I can,' I said. It was alcohol talking: I wasn't licensed to drive.

I grabbed the key, jumped in and started the engine. My mate was next to me in the front while three girls huddled on the bench in the back. I was full of confidence – I had driven cars that belonged to older friends through the bush and across paddocks, but never on the road – but I was just as smashed as all the others in the car. Making matters worse for my intoxicated mind was the fact that the jeep was a manual – I had to change gears, and I'd never done that before. Still, I did manage to figure it out and bunny-hop my way out of the yacht club car park unscathed. A few minutes later, I was driving the jeep quite fast down a hill towards the main road, when as we crossed an intersection someone shouted: 'Turn right here!'

I reacted instantly, turning the wheel as quickly as I could – which of course was a stupid thing to do at 70km/h (43mph). In a flash, the Suzuki went from being a car to being a roller coaster. I'd rolled it, and as we went over the windscreen exploded and sent shards of glass in every direction. I'll never forget the deafening noise of metal grinding into the tarmac and the screams from the girls. I expected the worst but – don't ask me how – everyone survived and no one was injured.

I'm not really religious, but this did seem like a miracle. How could five people – none of whom was wearing a seatbelt – walk away unscathed after rolling an open vehicle on a corner at high speed. The car was totalled, but there was not a scratch on anyone. It was beyond belief: it was as if we were blessed!

My mate broke the silence. 'Fuck, what have we done?' I just stood there stunned, staring at what was once a jeep. 'Spithill, we've got to get out of here – quickly, mate!' said someone.

We left that no-good heap of metal in the street and ran off in shock. One of the girls was crying, and justifiably so. About a kilometre away we came across a vacant taxi, so we all piled in, but we weren't sure of our destination until my mate remembered we were meant to be going to the after-party, so gave the driver the address.

After having a couple of settling beers at the party, everything that had just happened seemed like a weird dream. But it wasn't.

The next day I had to face the owner of the car, and it turned out that we had a bit of an issue: his car was a write-off and he didn't have any insurance. He presented me with an easy solution: pay him the value of the car – 5,000 bucks – and we'd all forget about what had happened.

Fortunately, I had been working relentlessly after school and during holidays as a labourer on building sites and at the local petrol station filling up cars with my good mate Justin Purll. (The latter occupation led to us being able to use a unique pick-up line with girls: we were 'petroleum transfusion technicians'). Through blood, sweat and tears I had actually managed to save just over $5,000 doing those jobs – $5,000 that was meant to be put towards my own boat. It was a shitload of money to me, but I had no option but to use it for something else. I had to pay for what I had done. There was no way I was going to shy away from my responsibility. I had been the driver so now I had to face the music. There was one rider to this settlement: no one was allowed to tell my parents.

I had a big series coming up the following weekend, but I found it impossible to prepare for it physically or mentally. The accident was gnawing away in my mind and I had plenty of sleepless nights.

On the morning of the race my dad could see something was troubling me.

'What's wrong, son?'

'Nothing Dad. Everything is all right.'

Thankfully he was clever enough not to push a gloomy teenager too far, but our result in that series laid me bare: I wasn't the Jimmy Spithill everyone knew. It was one of my worst efforts in all the years I'd been racing. We had dominated the competition all season, so we were the favourites to win, yet we finished up not even qualifying for the semi-finals.

My old man could sense that I was going through a storm, and he couldn't let it lie.

'What is going on? Why don't you tell me? I could help you.'

'Last Saturday, remember the yacht club party?'

'Of course.'

'Afterwards I totalled the Suzuki jeep.'

'Oh.'

He was silent for a few seconds, assessing what I had just said.

'Anyone hurt?'

'Nah.'

'Thank God. Now I get it. Now I understand why you didn't win that regatta; it was obvious that something was wrong. Were you drunk?'

'I am too young to drink.'

'That's not what I asked. Were you drunk?'

'Yep, legless.'

'What you did is one of the stupidest fucking things I have ever heard of in my entire life.'

I knew this was Dad speaking from the heart and from experience: he had been an alcoholic, and he'd driven cars when drunk but fortunately never had an accident. He realised the error of his ways. This was now his chance to straighten out his irresponsible teenage son.

'You've got to see this as a huge lesson. You could have killed a few people, which probably wouldn't have been that bad if you had also died, because at least you wouldn't have had to live with the fact that you killed someone else. But could you imagine what your life would be like if someone had died and you had lived on?'

He didn't yell at me, he never has, but what he said really shook me. So I lost my life's savings paying this guy for his dilapidated old jeep. It was a lesson learned: I dodged a bullet.

Some of Life's Lessons

My mid-teenage years on the 'mainland' were full of highs and lows, and in hindsight I realise I could quite easily have found myself on the wrong side of life. I think this was due in part to me experiencing the 'bad things come in threes' syndrome: my parents split up, the sailing programme stopped and the boxing gym closed. This all meant I had too much time on my hands and too little to do, until I started hanging around with the wrong bunch of guys.

The root of this problem stemmed from the fact that many of the kids I was going to school with came from broken homes, so they lacked parental control and role models. For this reason we were drawn to each other – a motley bunch of schoolkids who hooked up with others of a similar age and with similar circumstances ... and I was one of them.

Just about every day we would go in search of what we considered fun – fellow 'surfies' who also liked skating and riding BMX bikes. But many of these same kids also amused themselves by using drugs, getting into fights and committing petty crimes.

Such was the bond between us that we would just about crawl over broken glass to support each other if we had to – but instead of funnelling our energy into something useful, we'd be getting into trouble. There would be fighting at night, pinching drinks from shops, stealing other kids' bikes and the occasional act of vandalism. In addition to finding it fun, you kept doing it because you either became addicted, or were too scared of what your 'mates' would think and do should you choose to walk away. In reality, there was great energy and talent just going to waste. Some of these guys were awesome athletes, but they lacked the focus or discipline needed to apply it in the right direction.

For some reason I found myself becoming one of the pack, but I did my best to stay on the fringe because I didn't agree with what the worst guys were doing. That said, I thrived on hanging around in a gang and experiencing the strength of the bond that came via the brotherhood – a bond that meant that if a mate found himself in a confrontation you'd step in to help him. I certainly didn't like the drugs and the petty crime, though – for me they were fake thrills compared with the real excitement anyone can enjoy through sport and so many outdoor activities.

I accept that this was part of growing up and I'm happy to say the experiences contributed to me being where I am today. Yet at the same time I realise just how easy it would have been to get on the wrong side and never recover, or to be injured for life as a consequence of a confrontation.

There is one incident from this part of my life that I'll never forget – one that I hope carries a message for many young people. It happened one night when our group was having a drinking party in an isolated part of the Northern Beaches. A rival group showed up unexpectedly and, not surprisingly, a fight started almost immediately. At one stage a guy was pushed over, and as he fell backwards on to the ground he cracked his head open on the kerb. Although he survived, he suffered serious brain damage. The boy who pushed him finished up in juvenile detention. Two lives shattered in one instant of avoidable brawling.

It's disappointing but not surprising that many of the kids from that era were unable to get off that one-way track leading to bad times. Deep down they were good guys, but through a lack of guidance they let themselves be drawn into the dark side to a point where they couldn't – or didn't want to – find a way out. Of course they had choices along the way, but not everyone has the right items in life's toolbox to be able to convert wrong to right.

It was during this turbulent period that one of my most important and valuable life-changing experiences occurred. My father was on a bus heading to North Sydney where he worked when he noticed a sign for the North Sydney Police Boys' Club. When Dad came home that night he told me what he had seen.

Suddenly it was like the sun was coming up on a bright new day for me: a boxing club! Here was the opportunity I so desperately needed, the one to get me away from the local world of fake thrills and give me the chance to start afresh.

At the first opportunity I was on a bus and heading to North Sydney for what would prove to be a much-needed game changer. From the moment I walked into the club I felt comfortable in the environment. Old and new photographs and posters around the walls confirmed the club had had a wonderful history since its formation in 1937. I joined there and then and booked my first training session, which, as it would turn out, reinforced one of my earlier lessons in life. While I was standing there waiting to start training, two muscle-bound guys covered in tattoos from head to foot walked in. They looked as if they had just escaped from jail – the sort of guys you would never want to confront in a dark alley. They were there to box, but from the moment each one stepped into the ring it was obvious they couldn't throw a punch to save themselves. The guy they were matched with looked more like a nerd than a boxer – a skinny and lanky kid who wore glasses. But his appearance was deceiving … he was a wolf in sheep's clothing and he absolutely wiped the floor with not only them, but anyone else who dared enter the ring. Never judge a book by its cover, indeed.

I loved the hard training sessions, the relentless grind and the team spirit at the gym. It took me almost an hour and a half to get there each way by public transport, but that didn't deter me from going just about every night of the week.

One night was different, though. I had stupidly shared a joint with a mate before training – I have no clue why since I hated smoking weed; on the few occasions I'd done it it had made me feel lethargic and tired, but it obviously gave me Dutch courage because that night I was foolish enough to step into the ring. Man, did I cop a hiding. I finished up with a black eye and my ribs were sore for days. I haven't touched the stuff ever since. Another lesson learned.

North Sydney Police Boys' Club was a typical old-world sweat-scented gym. It had a couple of free-weight sections, a few exercise machines, a raised boxing ring and half a dozen punching bags. The brick walls were plastered with faded posters from legendary fights and the traditional one-liners, such as 'The harder you train, the luckier you get' and 'Only the fit are fearless'.

But what really made it unique for me came in human form – the trainer: Tony O'Loughlan, who would go on to coach the Australian boxing team. He became a mentor for everyone he coached; we all went to him for help and advice on how to improve our boxing, but in the process he gave us lifelong lessons on how to behave. This man was so good he had the psychological and human-relations skills to be able to simultaneously deal with 30 kids from different backgrounds. He taught us that no man is an island; that wisdom can come from anyone, even from a kid, but you must be clever enough to listen. On a personal note, I have to say, there's no knowing where I would have finished up in life had it not been for Tony and the North Sydney Police Boys' Club.

Tony was so inspirational that we would do anything for him, including devoting ourselves to training for two hours, four or five nights a week. This usually started with skipping ropes then progressed to shadow-boxing, which taught us the technical skills we could implement in a solid session of sparring. The final session involved punching the speedball and heavy bag and working with weights. It was a programme that certainly delivered results: that year, 1997, all the fighters in our club went undefeated, and I was among them.

Unfortunately, my parents couldn't be there for what was my first ever fight, which actually pleased me because Mum in particular freaks out at the idea of someone punching her son. But a bunch of my mates from school, and my grandad, made the effort to be there. My opponent was tough – a street-fighting brawler – so it promised to be an interesting contest.

Before the start of the first round I could hear my mates shouting 'Come on, Spithill', but as soon as the bell sounded I was oblivious to it all. It quickly became apparent that my opponent was hitting me everywhere – his target area was way out of whack. The only mistake I made – which I quickly corrected – was backing straight up instead of changing angles when he was attacking. This let him get me on the ropes a couple of times, but my defence was good and my counter punches were much sharper than his. I managed to knock him down in the third round, much to the delight of my rowdy mates, who had even more to cheer about a short time later when I was declared the winner on points by unanimous decision. My bout was also recognised as the fight of the night. Bringing added sweetness to the victory was the fact that my opponent's trainer was a guy named Johnny Lewis, trainer of six world champions, including a few legends: Jeff Fenech, Jeff Harding and Kostya Tszyu.

I'm proud to say that soon afterwards I was named Junior Fighter of the Year, and this led to Tony telling me I had the potential to make it to the Australian Olympic Team if I was willing to dedicate myself.

In the end, though, I chose sailing, one reason being that boxing has such a short 'use-by' date. I didn't want to risk ending up being punch-drunk after what would be a relatively short career. One of the great things about sailing is that you can spend your life enjoying it, but that's not the case if you're a boxer. Boxing did, however, contribute greatly to my ability as a sailor: it made me so much more alert and improved my ability to make split-second decisions. Both sports are all about 'now' – if you are not in the 'now' zone you get beaten. Because of this, boxing is an integral part of the team's training today and I love the sport.

* * *

At this stage in my life I was in a 'purple patch', as good fortune was with me. While I was still enjoying my boxing, the youth development programme at the Royal Prince Alfred Yacht Club kicked back into gear – so I was training at the boxing club almost every night of the week and sailing all weekend. And there was more: I was playing rugby, cricket and Aussie rules at school during the week.

At that age, I could not have wanted a better lifestyle.

Our sailing programme had by then expanded to include the larger, three-person Elliott 5.9 mini keelboats. The club had purchased six of them, so our coaches developed a scheme whereby they were trying various crew configurations. This was being done for a purpose: the top crew would go to the Australian Championship, and that would be followed by an international series in New Zealand – the unofficial Junior World Match Racing Championship.

At the end of the selection series one of the club officials went up to my dad.

'James is going to New Zealand.'

'Thanks for selecting him.'

'He selected himself: he won every race.'

We went on to win the series in Australia and twice in New Zealand. Consequently I was named Australia's Junior Yachtsman of the Year.

There was also good news for me at home. My old man had sorted himself out and become dry, which meant that he and Mum had also come to terms. I know it was not easy for them to get back together, but fortunately for us kids they did. Ever since then they seem to have been enjoying the 'happily ever after' stage of life. Despite this, they did have a bit of a problem: my academic progress, or lack thereof. My extreme focus on sport simply left no energy or time for academic endeavours. Fortunately, though, the school principal calmed them down, saying: 'Don't worry about James. With that positive attitude he will succeed in whatever he does. Not everybody needs straight As from university.'

Apart from sailing, there was one facet of high school that I really cared about: the rugby grudge match between Pittwater High and our arch rival Barrenjoey High, an event that was the annual highlight for both current and former students. Every year, nearby Newport Oval was packed with spectators, including plenty of past students, all desperate to cheer or jeer from the first whistle until full time. For me, as a player, there were additional incentives to do my best – it was my final year at Pittwater High, and it was also my 17th birthday. So, I was determined that the huge birthday party I was going to throw at home following the game would also be a victory celebration.

Mum had other thoughts on the matter, warning: 'Don't play the grudge match; you will break your arm.' To which I in my wisdom replied, 'Yeah, right, Mum.'

Both Dad and the school's sailing master, Peter Mulholland, were also against me playing because we were heading to Mooloolaba, north of Queensland's capital city, Brisbane, for the Australian teams' championship the following week. That was a big deal – we had won everything that there was to win in New South

Wales that year, so of course everyone was hoping we would also claim that championship.

But at my young age I knew everything, so I wasn't going to listen to anyone.

My teammates and I hated losing anything to our rivals, so we were looking forward to dishing out a real hiding to Barrenjoey. We couldn't have played better in the first half of the game – doing everything I could to lead by example. But sure enough, just before half-time, I found myself at the bottom of a ruck and – SNAP – I'd broken my right wrist!

'Hey coach, have you got anything for this?'

'Nah, we don't have anything – no bandages, no tape, nothing.'

Luckily, one of the local plumbers in the audience, an ex-student of Pittwater High, had a bit of electrical tape, so we could create a crude splint for it. Everyone tried to talk me out of continuing.

'Come on, Spithill, you can't play like this...'

'Spithill, that is madness...'

'Spithill, I am telling you, you may not enter the field again with your arm in that state.'

I let the comments from the coach and the teachers run like water off a duck's back, and checked that the tape stayed in place by rotating my arms a few times. It hurt like hell, but there was no way I was going to quit, especially since the score at that stage was tied! 'I'll be fine, Coach – can't even feel it,' I said, then lowered my voice, so that he had to lean towards me a bit: 'I don't care what you say, see if you can stop me.'

However, in the end it turned out it wasn't worth it. Not only did we lose the game, but also my wrist was never really the same again. I have no problems with boxing or sailing, but certain movements have been impossible since then. For instance, I can't arm-wrestle – though I think I will be able to go through life without arm-wrestling.

When Peter Mulholland found out that I had broken my arm, he was in tears. 'You are the captain of the team, and here you are with a broken arm. All is lost,' he lamented. To which I replied: 'No worries, Mr Mulholland. Look, I've got a waterproof cast and some painkillers – problem solved!'

And so it was. I sailed for four days in the National Championship with my arm in a cast, and our three boats excelled, performing so well that Pittwater High finally became the 1997 Australian High School Sailing Champions. As well as winning away from home, we completely dominated the series. We were on fire. I'm not going to lie, though; my arm hurt like hell, but I had to grin and bear it. I couldn't afford to lose face to the old man and Mulholland. Every time they asked about my arm I just smiled and replied: 'can't even feel it.'

As my final year at school was coming to an end, I started hanging out with a group of guys who are still among my best mates to this day: Shannon Pilon, Pat Elsegood, Nathan Thomas, Justin Purll and 'Greggos' Berry.

We still managed to get into trouble sometimes as only boys our age could, but compared with the previous crowd, it was innocent fun. On the odd occasion, at 2am, we had the ability to upset an Italian guy who lived nearby, so much so that he would come out in his undies and chase us down the street while brandishing a rake. Then there was my 18th birthday party, which I shared with Shannon (our birthdays were one day apart so we celebrated together). For the event, we borrowed a small sailing dinghy from school, having told the teacher we were going sailing. In fact, we wanted to use it as a huge ice bucket, and it was duly filled with ice, alcohol and other drinks for our party, which we held at the local surf club. Once we had emptied the dinghy by drinking everything we decided to further entertain ourselves by using it as a slide down the stairs to the foyer. Worse was to come. Soon after the party, some mates decided to paddle the same dinghy across nearby Narrabeen Lake. It sank not far from shore so they had to 'abandon ship' and swim back – it turned out that the hull had been holed when we were using it as a slide at the surf club. The dinghy was lost for good, but what a voyage.

Shannon's dad, Owen, was the local fire brigade captain for 32 years, and a bit of a legend in the region, a real hardman. In fact, both of Shannon's parents are the hardest-working, most honest folks I have ever met. One day, Shannon, Pat, Nathan, Greg, Purller and I were mucking around at Shannon's place, emptying the fridge of beer while hanging out in the kitchen. We were all about to get our driving licences so the talk was about cars and motorbikes and the crazy stuff you could do with them.

Owen, overhearing us going on about speeding cars and crazy manoeuvres, asked us to join him in the lounge room. 'OK, boys, I want you to come in here and watch something.' He sat us down in front of the video unit and started playing these videos that had been shot when his brigade had been called out to really bad accidents. 'Start looking at this,' he said, 'People mangled up – kids too – some of them dead.'

Our hot testosterone-filled cockiness was immediately transformed to cold shock. The silence was profound. 'Yep, a drunk driver caused that,' he continued. 'Fast-forward to the next clip. Family going too fast. Next clip. Motorcycle guy, leaned in too far going into a corner; hit by an oncoming car.'

It went on and on. None of us said a word. It was probably completely illegal to show us this truly horrible film, but it was the best thing Owen could have done. It was his way of getting the message about safe driving across to us know-it-all teenagers who were on the threshold of adulthood, and to whom he had given many great lessons during our formative years. I wish it were possible for these hard-hitting clips to be shown to all teenagers today. That would certainly help lower the road death toll!

My wife and I named our first son Owen.

Mixing It with the Silver Spooners

I was born James Spithill and stayed that way for all my younger years, and am to this day James to the family. At school, James didn't sit comfortably with my mates, though, so I was called Spithill. 'Jimmy' didn't emerge until my late teens when I was sailing in an international regatta with my good friend, Michael Coxon. For some unknown reason, he started calling me 'Jimbo', and others soon picked up on it. But 'Jimbo' then morphed into 'Jimmy', and that's me today.

About the time I was retitled 'Jimmy', something happened that really made me feel like fate was looking out for me. I was working casually as a builder's labourer on Scotland Island not far from home and a couple of us were digging trenches for the foundations of a house. It was tough going: all manual, no machines, but even so, it was still the kind of labouring I loved. Sweat was streaming down my back as I firmly hacked my hoe into the heavy clay. My mate Mick, who lived on the island, had a plaster cast on his broken wrist, so I was doing the harder stuff while he was doing the easier work – shovelling dirt into the wheelbarrow. While the kookaburras sitting in the trees above filled the air with their deep-throated 'laughter', I lifted the hoe above my head for the umpteenth time and hammered it into the ground. Then there was a shout of terror...

'Fuck, Spithill! What do I do? What do I do? Help me!'

'What are you on about, mate?'

At first I thought he was just mucking about, but then I suddenly realised he was genuinely alarmed about something. I wiped pearls of sweat from my eyes so I could get a better view of what was causing him such panic – it was a fat funnel-web spider – one of the deadliest spiders in the world!

Fear filled Mick's eyes. He was holding his broken arm away from his body and I could see the spider sitting halfway along the cast – black against white. Funnel-webs are not huge – this one was perhaps 5cm (2in) long – but he was very angry. He was up on his back legs with his fangs out, fangs so powerful they can pierce a toenail. He was ready to attack.

Having been raised in this part of Sydney I knew all about funnel-webs. They are fast and fatal. I wanted to say very calmly 'Don't move', but the words got stuck in my dusty throat. Then came the miracle – a flash right in front of Mick and me! One of the kookaburras that had been perched high above us on a branch of a eucalyptus tree swooped down like a dive-bomber, snapped the spider into its beak and flew back into the treetops. Just like that! Mick and I were in a state of disbelief. It was as if we'd seen an act of God: one bird's meat is another man's poison.

'Fuck, did that really happen?'

Mick was staring at me, incredulous.

From that day on we always shared our lunch with the kookaburras.

Brushes with deadly spiders aside, I love blue-collar work – the life of labourers. I was roped into it as a kid when my dad decided to convert our one-bedroom shack in Elvina Bay into a simple but respectable three-bedroom house. Back then it was always a competition between us: how many big concrete blocks could you carry in a day, or how many sandbags could you tote up the hill from the jetty.

The old man was pretty impressive; so impressive he would go through heaps of labourers simply because they couldn't keep up with him. If they were slackers he'd tell them not to bother turning up the next day, but on many occasions they wouldn't show anyway because his work ethic had broken them. He didn't employ a building company – he was doing it all himself. But then came Cal. He was big and strong, to the point where he worked non-stop every day alongside the old man. Between them they would do the work of four blokes, and they loved it. Incredibly, Cal couldn't read, write or tell the time – but holy hellfire, could he work. He'd break most men.

When I started labouring as a young man, Cal was the person I emulated. I was at my best when I was working alongside strong guys and just going for it. Sometimes we didn't stop all day – we went from start to finish without a break. The stamina, the workload, the relentlessness, the work ethic – it really follows the same pattern as in sport: hard work and dedication. Being so young, I often copped shit from the older blokes, but when you didn't back off, and kept coming back for more in the toughest of times, then you were quickly adopted into the 'family'. It's how hard you work that matters: what you do makes you an equal or an outsider.

One of my first employers was 'The Rock' – Peter Ball – an amazing character whom I more than admire to this day. I worked for him in his landscaping business for $8 an hour, which was a small fortune for me in those days.

He was in his late 70s when he retired as a 'recluse bachelor' to a small waterfront property up the Hawkesbury River. He was always eccentric, but by the time he decided to quit working I'm sure he and the aging Howard Hughes would have enjoyed a conversation. He is still a sporting tragic: he has lived for sport, either as a participant – he was a premiership-winning rugby player – or as a spectator. His life has been a departure from the norm in almost every sense: he shared his small house with a three-legged cat, a black cockatoo and a wild possum that came to the kitchen window every night for a feed. One thing you couldn't do was ask Peter if his beer glass was half full or half empty – it was always full! From the time he poured his first beer early in the day until he went to bed, he topped up the glass after every sip. I found The Rock to be so unique and special that I made sure I went up the river in my speedboat every time I was in Sydney just to see him. I found him to be a great 'leveller'.

* * *

'James had a meteoric rise in sailing' is a statement that I often hear, but the fact is that none of my success has come without an enormous amount of commitment and effort, along with a great team. Yes, I did really well in the youth events when I first started one-on-one match racing, but even so, graduating to the World Match Racing Circuit was a huge step. We certainly did not start at the top – our series placings when we entered that arena were, from memory, 10th, 14th, 8th, 6th … and sometimes we didn't even qualify for the main event. The victories didn't start coming until 2002.

Match racing is all about team effort, and the best thing I did in the early days was team up with Joey Newton. I have to say that if it weren't for Joey I wouldn't be where I am today. The crew rarely sees the limelight; they don't get the credit they deserve when it comes to our great victories. Match racing in general, and the America's Cup in particular, can be likened to the NFL where almost all the focus is on the quarterback, or to soccer, where it's on the goal scorer. In sailing it's on the skipper, which happens to be my position.

Joey grew up in Yeppoon, a country town 650 kilometres (400 miles) north of Brisbane, and we got to meet when we raced against each other at youth match racing regattas. We became mates almost immediately, and as our friendship grew, it became apparent to me that this guy from the bush not only had sailing talent, but was a team player who enjoyed having a beer and a laugh as well. Sometimes when there was an international youth regatta on Pittwater, Joey and his crew from Yeppoon would camp on the living room floor at home. This was great for two reasons: we could talk sailing and, of equal importance, when we went out at night Joey became a magnet for girls. He was the spitting image of Australian tennis great Pat Rafter, so it wasn't surprising that many of them thought he was the real thing. When that happened I went straight into character and started calling him Pat.

Back on the water, we can't remember if I asked him to start sailing with me or vice versa, but if it was Joey doing the asking, then I can only say it's one of the easiest questions I've ever had to answer. From day one, Joey and I have always sailed together, and have been members of six different America's Cup teams. We have also remained part of the international Match Racing Circuit during that time, our best year coming in 2005 when we won the Match Racing World Championship and every Grade 1 event we entered. We also achieved a feat that only Russell and Gilmour, to my knowledge, had done, and that was to go undefeated at a Grade

1 event, in Rome – from the round robins all the way through to winning the finals, without dropping a race. This was sailing with Joey, Michele Ivaldi, Magnus Augustson and Andy Fethers.

In the late 1990s to early 2000s the Match Racing Circuit was a huge deal for us, and we took it very seriously. It seemed that the dream I had when I was nine years old was already coming closer to being reality, step by step. Making this all the more exciting was that I already knew the Match Racing Circuit was how many of the great Cup sailors had got their start.

Our entrance to the 'big league' came in a fortuitous fashion via the European tour, which I did with Joey and two guys from Perth: Andy Fethers and Ben 'Bull' Durham. Initially, it was a catch-22 for us. To be invited to events you needed a ranking, and to get a ranking you needed to do events ... which we hadn't done. We got around this quite simply: we contacted the organisers saying that they could always call us if a spot became available through a team cancelling. After that, we crossed our fingers and hoped that call would come:

'Hi, this is so-and-so from the regatta starting this weekend. We have a cancellation, can you confirm your attendance?'

'Absolutely, we are on our way. Thank you!'

Then you had to be quick! Often these calls only gave us three or four days to get to wherever in the world the regatta was being staged. We'd just drop everything and order these cheap but changeable round-the-world tickets, because we never knew where we'd be going next. While competing at one regatta, it was always possible that we would get an invitation to another. So we'd go here, there and everywhere, until there were no more regattas available to us. That's when we would head back to Australia and I would return to labouring.

The hard grind made me realise that life often isn't fair: it was a hand-to-mouth existence, where we always had to do things on a shoestring budget. But what we lacked in dollars, we gained in self-esteem, and with that, a dogged determination to do well. The circuit was full of 'silver spooners', but I am sure our situation gave us an advantage in wanting success even more ... and with that, the boys and I developed an uncompromising attitude on and off the water.

We were also indebted to the old man. Since we didn't have any money, he would put our tickets on his credit card, which we knew he couldn't pay off. The only solution was for us to win some prize money to cover the fares and pay him back – which we always did in the end.

The boats are always identical on the Match Racing Circuit, so the emphasis was on the ability of the crew, to get the best out of the boat. Sometimes we'd get through to the finals and make a lot of money, while at other times we would make none at all. If we did very well, we might win US$10,000–15,000, but by the time we had paid our debts, including airfares and living expenses for five guys, it is safe to say we weren't getting fat.

To save money, especially on hotel bills, we lived out of our travel bags and couch-surfed in the homes of rival sailors or yacht club members. It was a real bonus for us if a regatta offered a deal that meant hotel accommodation was provided. But there was always the flight puzzle ... how would we get to regattas and back home for as little as possible, and on what airline? Returning to Australia on such cheap tickets invariably involved multiple stops, and a flight time of up to 45 hours with Aeroflot or some other lesser-known airline. I can't count how many hours we spent sleeping on airport floors while in transit.

Despite these difficulties, the big bonus for us was that things were going in the right direction; it took only a few events for us to be recognised as a promising young team from Down Under, and that often led to us getting a wild-card entry into a series without having to beg for it.

Among the events was the Cento Cup in Italy in 1999, which was a milestone for us, being the first Grade 1 Match Racing event to which we were invited to compete. Grade 1 meant the top of the sailing world. Finally, we got to race against the best – people such as Kiwis Russell Coutts and Chris Dickson, Americans Paul Cayard and Kenny Read and of course Australia's Peter Gilmour – guys I had heard about and idolised since I was a kid in Elvina Bay.

Not surprisingly, we were a bit star-struck in this illustrious company, but even so, we did pretty well by finishing sixth.

We loved to take on Peter Gilmour. He had sailed a few America's Cup campaigns, but never won. He was a multiple world champion in match racing, though, regarded as one of the top guys. 'Gilly' was known for his aggression on the racecourse – it was always full on, with fireworks from start to finish. I remember an Australia Cup race in Perth in which we were matched against him. There were multiple lead changes, collisions galore, penalties being issued constantly, and lots of screaming between boats and at the umpires. At the end of the match both crews were ruined. They just collapsed in the bottom of the boats, which were nearly ruined as well. Peter and I just smiled at each other as we crossed the line. It had been one hell of a race.

The team we admired most, though, was led by Russell Coutts, because he was the complete package when it came to match racing. He always surrounded himself with the best sailors, was very calm and collected. Apart from being a great sailor, his ability to maintain focus and composure under pressure were his greatest attributes. There seemed to be an aura around him every time he was on the water with his team.

* * *

I have always had to put in the hours – to the extent that while others were sleeping or having breakfast, I would be out on the water training, or would go running. For me that is the only way I can make the boat an extension of myself, something that enables me to make split-second decisions when they really matter.

This approach paid off, and success on the European Match Racing Circuit was convincing me that I was on the right course to achieve my ultimate goal – becoming a full-time professional sailor – and that inspired me to train even harder. But it was even more than being able to sail for a living. What I love is that when the start gun fires at a regatta, it doesn't matter who you are, what you are or how much money you have, the only thing that counts is who wants it the most.

SIX

The Door Opens to the America's Cup

My face was a nauseating shade of green, and the contents of my stomach were threatening to leave me at any moment. I was holding on to the steering wheel of the 50-foot ocean racing thoroughbred *Ragamuffin* and we were pounding our way south between Sydney and Hobart in the most heinous storm imaginable. The wind was gusting between 50 and 70 knots, and the motion of the yacht as it crashed over the waves was so violent it could only be compared to the worst-ever roller coaster ride – but in this situation, crew members were also cold, wet, hungry and seasick

I was literally hanging on for dear life in breaking waves that were sometimes more than 15m (50ft) high. This was the 1998 Sydney Hobart classic, one of the world's great offshore racing contests, and conditions had turned foul – by far the worst in the race's 54-year history.

Never was there a better example of the adage 'what goes up must come down'... *Ragamuffin* would burst through the top of a wave then free-fall 12–15m (40–50ft) into the trough that followed. The landing was so hard I was convinced that it was only a matter of time until her carbon-fibre hull burst wide open. Even though I was steering the yacht there was no way I could do anything but succumb to the instability in my stomach. I was seasick. Suddenly, I was delivering the remnants of the previous day's Christmas dinner to the Tasman Sea ... a very embarrassing circumstance for someone who had spent his life on boats. At the same time, my mind was alternating between two possible scenarios – a common process when you are really seasick. At first, you think you are going to die, which freaks you out, and then you realise that you are not going to die, which freaks you out even more!

Ragamuffin, along with the more than 100 other yachts in the 628-nautical-mile race, was in survival mode. We had only our very smallest sail – the storm jib – set, just enough to give us the steerage needed to negotiate our way over the mountainous waves, some of which would exceed the height of an eight-storey building. We had no option but to press on in those extreme conditions and as we did, I began to console myself with the thought that if any yacht in the race was going to make it, it would have to be the one I was steering. I was with possibly the most experienced crew in the race, with a total of well over 100 Hobart races between them.

I was doing everything I could to guide the yacht over each wave so that there would not be a thundering crash on the other side, but I was not always successful. At the end of my watch, Grant Simmer, 22 years my senior and one of the best sailors in Australia, came on deck, took one look at me and said with pity in his eyes: 'Shit, mate, head below and see if you can get some sleep.'

Grant and I swapped positions when *Ragamuffin* was in the valley of a wave. As he took the wheel I released the white-knuckle grip I had on it and gingerly made my way forwards towards the hatchway that would give me access to the accommodation below deck. Once there I began to think life on deck was actually better. With all hatches closed, the atmosphere was like a stinking, clammy sauna. It also looked like a bomb had gone off as anything that hadn't been stowed properly had become a projectile. Moreover, there was an element akin to water torture to contend with – drips were constantly finding their way below via leaky deck fittings. It reminded me of another old adage relating to what is actually a wonderful sport ... most of the time: 'The joy of ocean yacht racing is one of the world's best-kept secrets.'

Any thought I had of snatching even a moment of shut-eye proved to be fantasy. There was no way of sleeping in those conditions, so all I did was hope beyond hope that the life-threatening wind and seas would soon abate and we could continue on to Hobart in relative safety. Every 45 seconds or so you would experience a sensation of *Ragamuffin*'s bow pointing skywards and then, as she crested the wave, the bow would drop and descend like a dive-bomber in the following trough for yet another deafening landing that caused everyone off-watch to wince. All you could do was hang on and hope.

'I am supposed to be a sailor, what the fuck is going on?' I thought to myself.

Memories from my childhood came flooding back, reminding me of the time Katie and I sailed our little Manly Junior through a storm all the way across Pittwater so we could compete in a race, and how when we got there, the race had been cancelled because of the 'dangerous conditions'. All we could do then was sail home, and we did that without a worry in the world, even though the cold rain was pelting us like icicles and causing our eyes to sting. Now, here I was achieving another one of my childhood dreams – competing in the Sydney to Hobart race with some of the world's best sailors – and I was seasick. Making me feel even worse was the fact that just a few metres away the yacht's legendary owner, Syd Fischer, was in his bunk and snoring his head off.

After Grant and the lads had covered me for a few watches, it was my turn to go back on deck, and what I saw after I closed the hatch behind me and hooked on my safety harness was beyond comprehension. Both the wind and the waves had entered a new and terrifying league. The waves that were coming at us – they were more like breaking combers you see smashing on to a beach in a storm – were then averaging about 24m (80ft) in height. Some were even higher, and the wind, well it was just roaring at up to 80 knots. There was a constant and very real risk of a yacht being either capsized or rolled through 360 degrees by the combined forces of the wind and the waves. If that did happen we would almost certainly be dismasted, rendering us helpless and at the mercy of these horrific conditions.

Making this situation more dramatic was the knowledge coming to us via the two-way radio that yachts were in distress everywhere, but unfortunately there was little anyone could do about going to their assistance in a storm that was little different to a cyclone.

It wasn't long after I had gone on deck that I realised I had one small consolation – despite all this turmoil, I had overcome my seasickness. I don't know how or why, but I sure felt a lot better.

Most importantly, I was then able to effectively fulfil my role as part of the crew.

After being in survival mode for more than a day and a half, during which time only our tiny storm jib had remained set, we eventually got to Hobart. When we did we were shocked by what we heard. This horror race was overwhelmed by tragedy. Only 44 of the 115 starters managed to reach the finish line, 55 sailors were winched to safety and five yachts sank... Saddest of all, six sailors died.

The first yacht to finish was the American maxi, *Sayonara*, owned and skippered by Larry Ellison, the co-founder of software giant Oracle Corporation and the driving force behind our Oracle Team USA America's Cup campaigns. As an indication of just how awful it had been, his first words to the media when the yacht docked in Hobart were: 'Never again. That was a life-changing experience. It was a race for survival, not victory.'

It was certainly scary stuff. While *Ragamuffin* had the potential to win the race on handicap, seamanship and common sense combined to see us play it safe. We all agreed it wasn't worth risking your life for the sake of a trophy. As it turned out, we did manage to take third place on handicap but under the circumstances that meant little to us. Our thoughts were with the families of the sailors who had perished, and our thanks went out to the rescuers, especially the incredibly brave helicopter teams and, in particular, the paramedics who saved the lives of so many of our fellow competitors.

When back on dry land, the thought that I had let the *Ragamuffin* team down by being seasick haunted me day and night, simply because I hated not being able to pull my weight at that time. It was a feeling of guilt, so I promised myself that I would do the race again and not get seasick.

To my great disappointment, but not surprisingly, the fact that I had been seasick in my first long ocean race was soon common knowledge on the waterfront. The assumption being touted by these gossipmongers was that I would never be a winner when it comes to long offshore races. However, when I thought about it, I knew the best thing to do was prove the naysayers wrong. They reminded me of the bullies I knew back in my school days. So many of them scrambled to bring down good people via their harassment tactics and, more recently, through spreading vitriol online: it's really easy to be a tough guy when you are hiding in a basement in front of a laptop... I have thought about this a lot and am convinced that these people have significant shortcomings in their own lives and can't cope with other people's success. Sadly for them, bullies don't realise that they are the ones who lose out in the long run.

So, it was more important than ever for me to prove to myself – and my detractors – that I could get to Hobart without being seasick, and I have now done that on four subsequent occasions.

The most memorable of these races came in 2015, when I was part of the crew aboard the radical American maxi *Comanche* owned by Netscape founder Jim Clark and his Australian supermodel wife, Kristy Hinze Clark – who sailed with us. This was another tough Hobart race. Out of the 108 starters, 31 were forced to retire because of damage, including the race's line honours favourite and defending champion *Wild Oats XI*, which had on board two of my teammates from Oracle Team USA: Andrew Henderson and John Hildebrand. This was because before we had even reached the halfway mark we were hammered by what the locals refer to as a 'southerly buster', an extremely powerful and sudden change in wind strength and direction that comes out of the south, which nearly forced us out, too.

Worse was to come. Nine hours into the race, *Comanche* launched herself off a large wave and, on landing, the daggerboard on the port side fractured and threatened to carve into the carbon-fibre hull. Our only option was to cut it loose, but when we did that the remnants of the board washed aft under the hull and damaged the rudder. Our skipper, American sailing legend Kenny Read, made the tough call to retire from the race but, as we were limping north back towards Sydney, some of the crew led by *Comanche's* Aussie boat captain, Casey Smith, decided we should not give in unless all avenues for repairing the rudder had been explored. They got out their tools, disappeared below deck and somehow, quite miraculously, solved the problem. Thus *Comanche* rejoined the race after Stan Honey, our navigator, radioed in to race management.

Once back on track, we were able to pass *Rambler 88* (which had Oracle Team USA team mate Rome Kirby on board) and soon after we overhauled another maxi, the Australian entry *Perpetual Loyal*, leaving two more teammates from Oracle, Tom Slingsby and

Grant Simmer, in our wake. This of course gave me huge bragging rights inside Oracle Team USA. *Comanche* led the fleet into Hobart, just 2 days, 8 hours, 58 minutes and 30 seconds after leaving Sydney. This same race proved to be Syd Fischer's swansong. His 48th Hobart race was his last and, quite fittingly, *Ragamuffin* finished second across the line.

This was an important moment in my life. It was fantastic to realise a dream – I had gone from a little blue Manly Junior dinghy on Pittwater to being first to finish in the Hobart race aboard the world's most radical ocean-racing maxi. Further, I was able to prove the armchair critics and bullies wrong again ... I didn't get seasick!

* * *

So, how did a kid from Elvina Bay, who had virtually no money, get to be where I was at that moment in the 1998 Sydney to Hobart race, aboard one of the world's best yachts with one of the world's best crews?

The answer to this question was simple: the previous year I had been named the New South Wales Youth Sailor of the Year, while Syd Fischer had been nominated for Ocean Racer of the Year. Syd is a wonderful character who led by example; having started life with nothing, he went on to become a builder and, in turn, a millionaire. But it was his ability as a leader in business and in sport that set him above most others – his name and that of his yachts, all named *Ragamuffin*, were known and esteemed globally.

Back to the awards ceremony. Towards the end of the evening I felt compelled to introduce myself to Syd, a tough man I had always respected and one who had a reputation for being quite intimidating.

As I approached him all I could see on his rugged, chiselled face was what could only be described as a Dirty Harry stare. The conversation went something like this:

'Excuse me, Mr Fischer.'

'Yes.'

'Can I introduce myself? My name is James Spithill, and I am a match racing sailor and I am super keen to try some ocean racing.'

'I know who you are. I saw you on stage before. Congratulations on the award, mate. What are you up to on the weekend?'

'Nothing, Mr Fischer.'

'Stop the Mr Fischer bullshit. My name is Syd, and next weekend you can come out on Ragamuffin *if you are up for it. There's a regatta off Sydney Heads.'*

'You bet.'

'That's that then. See you Saturday morning. Seven o'clock. Don't be late.'

Unbeknown to me at the time was that Syd had already indicated to others in the room that he wanted to meet James Spithill, since he thought I was a good cut of a kid. But, more importantly, I had just met the man who would ultimately open the door to the America's Cup for me.

It was still dark when I got up that Saturday to go sailing with Syd. Luckily, our shitty old Ford Fairmont started – it often didn't – so that meant Dad could drive me the 30 kilometres (19 miles) from Mona Vale to Mosman Bay, near the city. Syd had *Ragamuffin* docked at his unique waterfront residence, which was obviously designed to accommodate his sailing lifestyle. His wharf was more like a marina, and a boating kid's dream: apart from the famous *Ragamuffin*, there were two 12-metre class America's Cup yachts and two America's Cup chase boats sitting idle at the dock. I soon located Syd and his crew, including his tactician, yachting great Grant Simmer – the tactician aboard *Australia II* for the historic America's Cup victory in 1983 – who would also play a significant role in my life in the years to come.

Within a few minutes of arriving, I was aboard *Ragamuffin*. It took us more than an hour to prep the boat, then we cast off and motored out of Mosman Bay and headed for the start line just off the entrance to Sydney Harbour. As we went I became entranced by the sound of the bow wave whooshing away from the sleek hull. I was hearing the soundtrack of my life.

Incredibly, Syd put me to the test from the outset. The race had only just started when he stepped away from the wheel, pointed at it then pointed at me.

'Go for it.'

'OK, Mr Fischer!'

'Fuck the Mr Fischer, Jimmy. Syd's my name; we're on an even keel.'

It was too good to be true: there I was steering the famous *Ragamuffin* within minutes of the start of my first ever ocean race! I did everything I could to conceal my excitement and act 'normal', but I'm sure my look of amazement and my smile, which spread from ear to ear, gave me away.

I must have done something right, because we ended up winning that race.

That day marked the start of a fantastic antipodean summer of offshore sailing for me, racing aboard *Ragamuffin* almost every weekend. At 19, I was the youngest on board by a considerable margin, and this led to Grant jokingly reminding me that I was 'too bloody young' to be the skipper of a 50-footer. Much to my delight, though, I held my spot in the team and this led to me experiencing great racing out of Sydney, as well as the 1998 Kenwood Cup regatta in Hawaii. That was something very special.

Syd had a reputation for being as tough as teak, and he was that to a degree, but it never worried me. He obviously liked my ability as a sailor, but he was sure I needed some strong guidance in life to reach my full potential. Of all the great things he taught me, there is one 'Syd-ism' that sticks with me to this day: 'If a bloke's good, you'll see it straight away.'

Syd was an astute businessman. Before getting into sailing he was the super-fit guy who played competition rugby in winter, and in summer handled the sweep oar in surfboat races on Sydney's ocean beaches. He also got into boxing but, like me, dropped it because he had no desire to finish off his life in the ring. This was the time in his life when he became a builder. Success led to success for him, and before long he had established Australian Development Corporation, a company that would build high-rise commercial and residential buildings across the city.

Syd was always good at striking the right deal, and this was never more evident than when he bought Sydney City Marine, a large waterfront facility perfectly situated in the western part of Sydney

Harbour. Syd acquired this property when the previous owner filed for bankruptcy, and Syd's company has since turned it around to the point where it is now one of the city's most successful marinas.

For me, a lot of Syd's guidance was given on land. When I left high school, he offered me a job looking after his boats docked at his home. It was hard work but I loved it because I was in my element – around boats. A typical conversation went like this:

'Jimmy, if you are in it, you have to give it everything you got. If you are out, you're out. If you want to be a professional sailor, you need to know everything. You need to know how to run boats, how to fix them, the whole thing. And even though you may be steering on the weekends, you have to start from the bottom. Too many of the skippers out there are wimps and know fuck all about how a boat comes together.'

'Right-o, Syd.'

'Remember you can be a rooster one day and a feather duster the next.'

Syd went through a lot of guys, getting rid of them as soon as they started slacking. I think I lasted the longest in a job that involved the basic stuff – anything from sweeping the floors to maintaining equipment that came from *Ragamuffin*, the old America's Cup boats, a barge, the chase boats and small runabouts. The hours were long and the work relentless; it was just never-ending. Scraping barnacles, painting, grinding, sanding, repairing, resealing, rigging – we did the lot.

Syd was tough, but fair. He wanted to give me an opportunity – a lesson in life. He'd come up the hard way and learned that success isn't easy. I am sure that is what he wanted to instil in me: there were no shortcuts when it came to getting to the top. Perhaps that is why I was only paid 150 bucks per week, even though he was running a multi-million-dollar company. It never occurred to me to complain, though. Why should I? I was surrounded by boats all the time and was learning heaps, I met fellow sailors, and I got to race on some of the world's best boats at the weekends. I loved every minute of it and I wanted more.

While I was racing *Ragamuffin* and working on the boats, Syd was trying to get his fifth America's Cup programme underway.

I could only admire him. Here was a bloke who had hardly been aboard a yacht before he was 30 now going for the top. Initially, he hadn't been able to see the sense in taking so long to get a boat ready to sail, when, in a matter of minutes, you could be filled with the excitement that came from a surfboat charging down an ocean wave. But he had obviously mellowed with age. One day, a friend convinced him to be part of his crew for a race on Sydney Harbour ... and the rest is history. Syd is now one of the most highly decorated offshore sailors in Australian history. He kept going until 2016, when he retired from sailing at the ripe age of 89. His remarkable involvement in five America's Cup campaigns led to him being inducted into the America's Cup Hall of Fame in 2017.

Big Hopes, Small Bucks

Choppy and chilly, grey winter waves were splashing across my neoprene-covered body while I was hanging over the side of the heeling hull of a 27ft Soling – an Olympic class three-man keelboat designed for speed more than comfort back in the mid-1960s. Through the Perspex window in the mainsail I caught a glimpse of the jagged profile of the roof of the Sydney Opera House, then a few seconds later my father came into the frame, off to leeward and standing in a small powerboat. This wasn't unusual really, since he was my number-one supporter, but he was also there to lay marks so we could practise starts and mark roundings. Sometimes I wonder how many thousands of hours he has spent over the years helping my sister, brother and me to pursue our passion for sailing – and winning…

That day, we were out on the water so we could train against another Australian crew led by sailmaker Gary Gietz and a team from France led by Philippe Presti – who would play a huge ongoing role in my career. We were all there for one purpose – to qualify for the 2000 Olympics in Sydney.

When I took a second glance at Dad I noticed that he was on the phone, and as it turned out the conversation he was having would soon lead me to a more exciting experience than being at the Olympics.

'G'day Arthur, it's Syd.'

'Hi Syd. What a surprise to get a call from you! What's up?'

Dad's reaction to Syd's call was understandable. Even though he was my unofficial sailing manager at that early stage of my career,

Syd would not have contacted him more than six times – so Dad immediately sensed this was going to be no ordinary chit-chat, and it wasn't!

'Look, I've got this mate called Ian Kortlang, and he reckons the best way to get an America's Cup team together would be to make it into a kind of youth challenge. We'd use Sydney 95, the boat built for my last America's Cup campaign, and call it Young Australia. I want Jimmy to skipper it with a crew from the Youth Match Racing arena. What'cha reckon, Arthur?'

'That sounds fantastic, Syd. I reckon it's a great idea.'

'Right-o. Tell Jimmy, would you? I'll discuss it more with him at work on Monday.'

When I arrived at work at Syd's place the following Monday, he was waiting for me, as was Ian Kortlang.

'Look, Jimmy, if you can get a good young team together for this campaign you can have Sydney 95. I've already found a shipping sponsor who will transport it across to Auckland, and I've no doubt we can raise some sponsorship dollars. So ... are you up for skippering an America's Cup boat?'

Does a kangaroo like jumping? Can a redhead fight? It was a no-brainer. Who cared if the boat was so slow that it came last in the previous America's Cup?

'Am I up for it? Of course! And I think it would be great to bring somebody like Rob Brown aboard to coach a campaign like this. What do you say about that?'

Syd thought about that for no more than two seconds.

'Sure. As long as you can do it within the shoestring budget, you can do whatever you feel is needed.'

I was 19 years old. This was a crazy opportunity that was beyond my wildest dreams – the chance of a lifetime to become part of the America's Cup scene. I was going to give it my best shot, but little did I realise that we were going to defy the odds in more ways than one.

Ian Kortlang, a well-spoken and imaginative spin doctor with thick, swept-back hair, was the man who was going to teach us the ropes in media and PR. I saw Syd and him as a bit of an odd mix – Syd was the kind of guy who would probably scoff down raw eggs for breakfast, while Ian would be having eggs Benedict. Not that he was a snob, he just knew the good life and how to enjoy it.

Syd somehow convinced Sir James Hardy to be a patron, which gave the *Young Australia* challenge some status. Jim was a bit of a living saint in sailing in Australia, but outside the yachting world he is probably better known in association with his family wine brand, Hardys. He and I to this day are great mates.

Also on side was Rob Brown, a kind of all-round sailing legend: multiple world champion in the 18ft skiffs; part of the winning America's Cup team in 1983; a childhood hero of mine; and always a tremendous campaigner. He was also a neighbour of ours in Elvina Bay, who had known me since I was born. In fact, it had been Rob who found some scraps of old sailcloth and made us the first spinnaker we used on that little blue Manly Junior.

Of course, we realised that Syd also had an ulterior motive; *Young Australia* was not only about giving some young blokes a chance. He had already put down a US$250,000 performance bond to be part of the America's Cup 2000, but he couldn't get the sponsors together for a full-on campaign. So, the *Young Australia* concept was his least expensive means of getting to the Cup and redeeming his US$250,000.

Word of the *Young Australia* campaign spread like wildfire across the sailing scene, so in no time we had some of Australia's best young sailing talent lining up to be part of the adventure. On Rob's advice, we did not use the America's Cup boat for the crew selection since we didn't know the capacity of all the applicants. It was not difficult for an inexperienced person to be killed on an AC boat – the loads on sheets, halyards and sails were enormous. Instead, so we could separate the young 'wheat from the chaff', we used the 50ft carbon-fibre *Ragamuffin* that had delivered us to Hobart safely.

Our selection process did not focus on sailing skills alone. The aspiring crew members also had to know how to be part of a team and not be prima donnas. Consequently, we didn't consider quite a few fantastic sailors because of their attitudes. Within a few days, though, we had a complete crew comprising 11 guys aged between 18 and 22, some of whom – Joey Newton, Andy Fethers and Ben 'Bull' Durham – would sail with me in future cup campaigns.

In this period of my life I learned the importance of patience and confidence. You've got to have patience with people when you are trying to build a team because you have to make sure all the right pieces fall into place. It was also interesting for me to realise that many of the guys stood by me because of my 'we can do it' attitude. This was probably the first time I really experienced the power of confidence; it's a force that can really tip the scales in your favour.

The following months were relentless: training on Sydney Harbour in the morning, trying to flog sponsorships in the afternoon and maintaining the boat in the evening. *Young Australia* was in a bad way and required some serious work. For a start, the entire hull needed to be strengthened, a task that would take an inordinate number of hours to complete. The good news was that the young guys we had selected for the team were full of enthusiasm because they were hungry for the opportunity to break into the America's Cup. Everyone knew what needed to be done, and they did it, even if that meant burning the midnight oil. Our pay cheques were laughable: I think I was getting about 200 bucks a week – possibly less – and the others 160 bucks a week. But we were living the dream.

Looking back, it was miraculous that we even got the *Young Australia* campaign off the ground. Fortunately, some sponsors came on board and I learned a lot, running a team and getting out there in the corporate world selling sponsorship: Toshiba gave us communication equipment and cold hard cash; Aerolíneas Argentinas gave us free flights from Sydney to Auckland where the Cup was being sailed; and Line 7 gave us sailing clothes and cash. The latter donation provided me with an America's Cup jacket with my name on it, and you can only imagine what that meant to me. The clothing was quite a step up from the maroon football jerseys we had to share with the rugby team at Pittwater High! Still, everyone was quite realistic about our chances … nobody expected us to win or get a top place. But for our sponsors, we were the youngest crew with the oldest boat and the smallest budget, and that appealed to them. We would get them plenty of attention. It was at this time that I realised that Ian Kortlang was a great spin doctor and an absolute genius at what he did.

Rob Brown turned out to be a godsend. He has such a good reputation that anyone and everyone was happy to lend a hand to a bunch of young, motivated sailors. He convinced mates to fix broken equipment for free, while his father, who was a fitter and turner, manufactured parts for us. Rob's wife was a graphic designer who did all the artwork and branding. Rob also managed to get some sail repaired or recut for no cost. Having said that, some of our sails were antiques … they were being hoisted for their third America's Cup!

We were the last team to arrive in Auckland. It was the end of June, just a couple of months before the start of the Louis Vuitton Cup, the series that decides who would challenge the defender (New Zealand) for the America's Cup. In those days, it was a round-robin series over three months in which all contenders raced against all of their rivals in an elimination process.

Unlike the other 10 teams, we had no base. On arrival, we did not even have anywhere suitable in which to dock our boat near the Viaduct Basin in Auckland, which was the 'pit lane' of the America's Cup. So, for us, it was a case of 'if you don't have any money, you have to be creative'. Rob and I soon found the perfect solution. It was called *Hikinu* – a 165ft-long, 100-ton barge with a towering blue crane on it. That meant we could haul the boat out of the water after each day's sailing and also have a base for our operations. Even so, we were blocked from docking this monstrosity anywhere near Viaduct Basin.

Fortunately I had a lifeline I could use: Sir Peter Blake, a Kiwi sailing legend, who had told me when I met him in Sydney during a fundraising event earlier in the year, to call him if I ever needed any help.

'Hey Peter, it's Jimmy Spithill. You've probably heard we don't have any money for a proper base, but we have found this barge, which we can have in the Viaduct in a couple of hours. But I am told they won't let us bring it in for obvious reasons ... we don't fit the America's Cup image.'

'Leave it with me, Jimmy.'

(Sadly, Peter is no longer with us. He was shot and killed by pirates off the coast of Brazil in 2001. I will be for ever grateful for the assistance he gave us and our campaign and, on a personel note, for being a mentor.)

Peter called Grant 'Guthrie' Davidson, who was responsible for the Viaduct Basin precinct. He was anything but over the moon about our request to allow the barge into the Basin, but an hour later, he, Peter and I were standing at the Basin entrance watching as our 165ft monstrosity was towed towards us. As it came closer, the captain of the diesel tug that was chugging away while pulling the barge gave one long blast on the ship's horn, as if in anticipation of success. This was not to be. Guthrie looked at us, scratched his bald head and wore a worried frown.

'No. You are not bringing that thing in here. No way. Forget it.'

'Ah, but come on, Guthrie – it's not that bad.'

The metallic horn blared again.

'No way. It ain't gonna happen.'

'All right mate, let's just tie it up and we'll talk about it.'

But as soon as we had it tied up, that was that – we decided we weren't going anywhere. As Guthrie and Rob were arguing, I went and untied the tugboat and told the captain to get out of there. Don't ask me how we got away with it, but this old grey thing with the big blue giraffe of a crane and a couple of shipping containers on the deck, which served as tool sheds, simply stayed put ... right in front of the brand-new, mega-expensive development where the other multi-million-dollar syndicates were based. Within minutes, the media had caught on to what was happening, and immediately the story got out about the youngest America's Cup crew with the oldest boat and the smallest budget. And even though we were Aussies, the story really hit home. We had people coming down to the dockside to donate pushbikes so we could get around, while old ladies brought us cakes and other food. Our unique circumstances, which meant we were the outright underdogs, saw us become the centre of attention for many in Auckland, so much so that whenever we threw a barbecue on the barge to thank our supporters, loads of people would turn up.

When it came to accommodation, Syd organised some low-budget, dormitory-style rooms for us on a local university campus. We were told it was far from flash, so most of the guys were saying things like, 'Shit, this will be terrible.' But when we got there, it turned out to be the greatest thing ever – the university was full of female European exchange students!

Suddenly, at age 19, I felt as though I'd woken up on a bed of roses. We had so much fun; fun that sometimes got a bit out of control ... to the point where Syd and a couple of our mentors decided that there had to be a curfew for the entire team. The rule was simple: 10 o'clock in your bed – on your own. But boys will be boys, and girls will be girls! Every night at 9.55 there'd be this hilarious scene in which all the dormitory doors would open and most of the girls would disappear back to their rooms. I say 'most of the girls' because when our mentors came in to check at 10pm there would be girls hiding under beds and in wardrobes, trying desperately not to giggle. We always did our best to get away with it, our theory being that because we were working so hard for so little reward, the only way to really stay sane was to party as hard as we could and make sure we had a lot of laughs.

The date 31 August 1999 was very memorable because that was when our party scene got even better: New Zealand changed the legal drinking age from 21 to 18, which meant that all us sub-21-year-olds could then go to the pub, and we did! Our regular 'watering hole' became The Loaded Hog, the best pub on the waterfront at Prince's Wharf in the Viaduct. It certainly stood out from the rest with its yellow façade, highlighted by a big red neon outline of a pig. The bartenders were great; they knew we didn't have a lot of money to spend, so on the odd occasion they would shout us a round of drinks simply because they felt they should look after us.

There was no hiding the fact that 'the young kids from *Young Australia*' were the poor relations of the America's Cup that year. It was well known across Auckland, and prompted a couple of the guys on the team to come up with a stroke of genius: they played the sympathy card. They figured out that if we wore our gear – crew jackets and shirts – at night, we could pretty much go to any bar and get free entry and free drinks. The scheme saw immediate success, so we decided to take it a step further ... we started calling various venues to get invitations to sporting events and concerts. It worked a treat and we soon found ourselves hosted in corporate boxes or sitting in some of the best seats in the house.

We were a bunch of young guys having a lot of harmless fun, but even so, we didn't lose sight of the fact that we were in Auckland to go sailing and do our best.

To put it mildly, when compared with the latest America's Cup yachts, ours was a piece of old junk. There had been a huge advance in technology between 1995 and 2000, and our boat belonged very much in the 1995 era. The hull shapes had gone from being very wide and resembling aircraft carriers to very narrow and spear-like. The mast and sail combinations had also developed dramatically, as had the keels and rudders. So, when out on the water, our boat sailed like a tank and the others like arrows. Moreover, it was not like *Young Australia* had been a winning boat when racing as *Sydney 95* in Fremantle five years earlier – it had come in last! But despite the odds, we managed to really embarrass some of the other teams in Auckland. In the first round robin we had only one win, but we won a big percentage of the starts by outmanoeuvring our more fancied competitors.

Every day we wished that the race were only about the start and the first 100 yards upwind. If that had been the case then we would have had a serious chance of becoming the challenger for the Cup. Dream on! Instead, the actual course was over 18.5 miles and comprised six windward/leeward legs with a downwind finish. We spent a lot of time looking at a lot of sterns when racing that year.

There were three round robins leading up to the semi-finals, and of course we got knocked out. However, of the 30 races we contested we managed to win four, which was seen by everyone as a commendable effort. The important thing was that we got out there and upset a lot of teams. Much to everyone's amazement, including our own, we even beat one team overall that had built a brand-new boat that was skippered by a triple gold medallist, the East German legend Jochen Schümann. We could have done even better, but we kept ripping sails and breaking equipment because everything was too old – except the crew! Our hull was also a contributing factor; it was slower than a school clock approaching recess.

After we got knocked out of the eliminations, Paul Cayard's *AmericaOne* team approached me to ask if I and some of the *Young Australia* crew would join that syndicate and sail their training boat against their race boat in practice sessions. Unfortunately for both sides, though, the rules stated that if you had been part of an existing team in that America's Cup series, you couldn't join another team.

So, we could only watch from a spectator boat as Paul Cayard's team went through an epic final series against Italy's Prada *Luna Rossa* that went to the wire. In the final winner-take-all race, the yachts were just metres apart for almost the entire distance, and the lead changed over and over again. *Luna Rossa* just managed to hold out *AmericaOne* at the finish and won the right to challenge for the Cup after winning 5–4.

This result marked an extraordinary moment in the America's Cup's 149-year history: never before had there been an America's Cup match without an American either defender or challenger. The Kiwis, led by Russell Coutts, went on to absolutely slam *Luna Rossa* in the finals, which meant that the following America's Cup would also be held in Auckland. But would I be there?

The time had then come for me to pack up, go home and see where fate would take me.

I flew out of Auckland knowing that everyone in the *Young Australia* team could hold their head high; we had beaten the odds and stood up to be counted. Prior to the event there were plenty of people saying it was dangerous for *Young Australia* to be out there – that we were in over our heads. But unlike many other teams, we never caused a collision and no one was injured. Also, I say with pride that everyone who was on the boat has gone on to do bigger and better things – winning major international offshore races and the America's Cup, becoming world champions, or seeing success in the yachting industry. On the flip side, disappointingly, many of the sailors who hadn't believed in us when we started the campaign and hadn't dared join the team later came looking for a job as soon as it became apparent what our next challenge would be.

For me, the hard part was yet to come. As it turned out, being involved in the *Young Australia* campaign nearly killed my America's Cup sailing career before it had properly started.

Kicking Down the Door to the America's Cup

'Hey Syd, why don't we do a real one – a real America's Cup challenge with a proper budget and a proper boat? The team has shown its potential – what we did with that old piece of junk in Auckland was pretty good.'

'Sure. OK. Let's try.'

It had been months since we had had that conversation. But since then, nothing. Worse still, every time I tried to broach the subject, Syd became increasingly vague. The fact was that he just couldn't raise any money in Australia for another America's Cup challenge. Syd may be a legend in Australian offshore sailing – he has done fantastic things with his string of yachts named *Ragamuffin* – but when it came to the America's Cup he simply didn't have the same status. Unlike his ocean-racing effort, he had never achieved a decent result in the America's Cup – and only winning brings in the big sponsorship bucks.

I really wanted to be part of a strong Australian challenge for the Cup, so for many weeks I was living in hope that Syd would get things moving. However, in the meantime, other America's Cup teams were reaching out to the boys and me with good offers to join them. None of us wanted to miss this chance, but time was running out. I needed a definite answer from Syd because it was then September 2000, and the challenging teams were already well advanced with their plans for the match in 2003.

It was time to talk to Syd before it was too late for all of us.

I was still working for him at his boatshed, and this particular morning, when I was doing some work at the top of the mast of one of the 12-metres, I sensed he was there. I hadn't seen him, I just felt his presence. The man has a remarkable aura around him.

I looked down from the masthead and, sure enough, I caught a glimpse of him out of the corner of my eye. I called on the guys to lower me to the deck so I could get to him before he disappeared into the city, where his office was located.

'Hey, Syd, can we have a talk?'

'OK, come inside. What is it?'

We walked inside the lower level of the Mosman shed and up to the second floor of his residence. As we went, I was rehearsing in my head what I was going to say to him. I knew this meeting could change a lot – including my entire life. If this meeting went as expected, I would be able to hand in my notice and finally become a full-time professional sailor. My lifelong dream would come true.

He had an office at his home, so we went in there, closed the door to escape the noise of the boatyard, and sat opposite each other. Straight away he grabbed a stack of papers that were on his big black desk and started eying them intently. He then looked up and said:

'So, what do you want, Jimmy?'

'Syd, it's been weeks since we talked about doing another America's Cup challenge. You have to make a decision if you want to do it or not because time is already running out. If you want to do it, I would be more than happy to do it with you. But then we've got to find the money.'

My statement was greeted with deafening silence. I hesitated before uttering the words I'd been rehearsing in my head for days.

'If you don't want to do it, then let the boys and me go – free us from our contracts. I don't want to sit around and wait without any answers because I have got some pretty good offers under my nose; I

have the chance of my lifetime here. To be honest, you have not taken a single step towards another America's Cup campaign, and that worries me.'

He lifted his eyes and looked through me. He said nothing for what was probably 10 seconds, but felt like an hour. The exchange that followed was as casual as if I had asked him if he wanted a cup of coffee. It went something like this:

'No.'

'No, what?'

'I'm not gonna let you go.'

'But you have nothing on.'

'I will not let you go. End of story. You are still under contract. I've invested in you and it's my decision.'

The other guys were essentially free to go. I was the only one Syd was interested in keeping locked in. Unfortunately, he had the upper hand because, legally, I was under contract.

At that stage of my life I knew everything I had worked for and desired was so close. It was a goal that I had worked so hard to achieve – it wasn't something that had been gifted to me. But now, if I wanted to become the professional America's Cup sailor that I'd dreamed about, I would first have to battle my way out of a contract with this guy. Amazingly, though, that didn't concern me right then. I knew I had a lot to fight for – in essence, my life. Instead of worrying about it, then, I reflected on what both my grandads had taught me: *'Never give up and always go out swinging.'* My next thought was simple: 'OK, fuck it – I'm going to go out swinging.'

Everyone I spoke to about my dilemma offered different advice, but there was one common thread – it would be a very rugged road if I took Syd on in a legal battle. I already knew that, but the overriding fact for me was the knowledge that I wouldn't get to where I wanted to be while Syd kept me locked into that contract. That meant just one thing: I would have the fight of my life on my hands.

Dad did his best to talk me out of tangling with Syd. He was well aware of the man's reputation when it came to court battles, so he was certain the odds were stacked against me big time. But I was sticking to my guns. 'No, I want to go for it,' I said. 'This is my only chance!' There and then Dad declared that he and Mum would stand by me all the way. I couldn't thank them enough.

I knew I wouldn't be able to get out of the contract on my own. I needed legal help, but I didn't know any lawyers. Then there was the small issue of money – I didn't have any, and my family was barely making ends meet – so how was I going to pay for it?

In response, I turned to the people around me, and I kicked a goal right from the start.

Jack Elsegood was a naturally talented and hard-as-nails rugby league player, and the older brother of one of my best mates, Pat. Jack had a well-connected agent, George Mimis, who represented a lot of Australia's top athletes, so after he heard my story he arranged for us to meet George.

The three of us went to dinner to discuss my dilemma. We weren't long into our discussion when we were joined by Peter Bobbin, a highly respected lawyer; when it came to legal warfare, he was the cavalry.

Peter soon concluded that there were some weaknesses in my contract when it came to restraint of trade, but the trump card was 'the lack of monetary consideration'. In layman's terms, a contract must contain two elements: what should be done, and how much money you should get for doing it. Apparently, the money part was a legal imperative – a contract had to have a monetary consideration.

However, my contract's consideration only read something along the lines of: 'In consideration of JS providing the services and loyalty aforesaid, he will be exposed to various aspects of yacht racing etc...' So Peter concluded that instead of being properly paid, I was getting little more than pocket money, and because of that, the contract I had should be regarded as null and void.

It sounded to me like it was a cut-and-dried case, but I was soon to learn that nothing in law is simple. There was a lot of work to be done since we had to prove every point with proper documentation. I wasn't at all surprised to hear this. For me, it was just like being in a regatta, where you cannot take any shortcuts when it comes to preparation.

Dad and I were soon burning the midnight oil in front of the computer and delving into filing cabinets. We had to go through old emails, letters and minutes from meetings – anything that related to the terms of my contract. So great a help was Dad that my non-religious mind was thinking: 'Thank God Dad is not drinking any more and can help me.' I would not have managed it without him.

My legal aid didn't come cheap. The lawyer charged typical inner-city legal fees, then I had to pay for opinions from a bunch of senior legal counsel and they, too, didn't come cheap. Bobbin's estimate for his fees and the opinions was in the region of $40,000! This was a huge problem for me. I knew the figure was fair in terms of the going market rate, and I believed Bobbin could win the case for me, but I simply didn't have any money. I was in a desperate situation and couldn't think of a way to fund this fight, until I discovered I had a support team willing to back me … Mum and Dad! While they had no cash readily available, they offered to extend their already stretched mortgage should that be necessary in order to guarantee the costs would be covered. In short, my parents put everything they had on the line to back me. I knew I couldn't let them down – and that made me even more determined to win.

There were plenty of sleepless nights for my parents and me while we were going through this legal battle. In a small way I knew how they felt, recalling how I had had to hand over every cent I had – $5,000 – to pay for that Suzuki jeep that I trashed a few years earlier. But there was added concern for me: the emotional burden that came from knowing I had my family's financial future in my hands. If I lost against Syd, I would have to continue working under the terms of our contract and make virtually no money, which in turn meant I would have no chance of repaying my parents. Tom sensed at this time that something was wrong within the family, but we did our best to keep the details from him.

There certainly were plenty of times during this unwanted experience when I wondered if it was all worth it; fighting Syd, putting everything on the line and risking just about everything my family had was nothing short of terrifying. But there was a concurrent thought: each time I considered my family and what Syd was trying to do to me I became intensely angry. With that came a steely commitment – I would not surrender. I would not let them down. I would not give up.

It was true that I had already been approached by most of the teams lining up for America's Cup 2003 in Auckland, and we had had conversations. The most serious proposal came from the American *OneWorld* team, whose skipper was Peter 'Gilly' Gilmour, another Australian sailing legend, and someone whom we had raced on the circuit and really respected. I remember taking the long bus ride from Mona Vale into the city to meet 'Gilly' for the first time to discuss the syndicate's proposal. Ironically, the meeting was at the Sheraton Hotel, adjacent to beautiful Hyde Park and about a block away from Syd's city office.

Gilly was adamant that the syndicate backers really wanted me on the team.

'Is there a way for you to get out of the contract with Syd?'

'Yes... I hope so.'

He also told me there was a deadline, because back then you had to have a distinct connection with the country of the team for whom you were racing. To sail for an American team meant I would have to have American residency by a certain date. He assured me that the *OneWorld* syndicate could sponsor me for all the things I needed, but added that we had to act quickly otherwise American immigration regulations could destroy the whole proposal. The six-figure offer that was put on the table left me in no doubt that my freedom was worth fighting for; it was potentially the ticket out of a financial crisis for my family and me. In an instant, any lingering doubts I had about going into battle with Syd vanished. I was ready to do what had to be done: go head to head with Syd.

Gilly and I drafted a deal literally on the back of a table napkin at the Sheraton. We agreed on the important points, but of course I couldn't sign anything while I was still under Syd's thumb. All I could do was promise Gilly I would get back to him soon and that I looked forward to joining the team and to the opportunity.

I left the Sheraton and walked down the street to Peter Bobbin's office. We discussed the meeting with Gilly and then I stressed there was even more reason than ever to win the case against Syd. Losing was not an option. If we failed, my family's home would go and I would not be able to pay Peter the full amount up front, as was required. I assured him that I trusted him and no matter what, I would eventually pay him back.

On Bobbin's advice we struck the first blow, suing Syd for the lack of monetary consideration in the contract. After a couple of weeks' silence Syd answered with a counter-suit towards me – for $1.7 million! That number was out of this world, and even though he'd pulled it out of a hat, it had the desired effect: it scared the living shit out of me – and Dad, who opened the letter. Now I was really losing sleep!

Syd claimed that he had invested $1.7 million in me, money that he would never get back if he released me from my contract. Given my weekly wage of $150, I have no idea how he came up with that figure. Syd also asserted that, even though I was a Match Racing Youth Champion before I met him, he was the reason for my success.

While the whole scenario was pretty disconcerting for a 20-year-old with no money who had put his parents' home at risk, the fact was that Syd had a weak case, and he knew it, due in part to the poor amount of documentation he had relating to my employment with him. I'm sure he also knew that he would have to spend a hell of a lot of time and money building a case that he would, most likely, lose … and he didn't like losing in business or in sport.

When Syd's legal team saw how well prepared we were for the case, and the firepower we had with Bobbin leading a well-respected legal team (including another lawyer, Peter Sardelic), they realised I meant business. I am sure they then began to understand that they were fighting a lost cause.

A month later Syd came back to us…

'Look, just give me $400,000, and we'll forget about it.'

Of course we refused, and I began thinking, 'When will this fucking nightmare end?' We knew the law was on our side, but that didn't guarantee us a win. These cases are often a war of attrition in which the big guys slowly let the small guys bleed themselves dry of all their resources – which was happening pretty damn quickly for me at that stage. It was time to go to court!

At this stage we were out of money, the bank wasn't going to lend us any more money and I was *all in*.

As Dad, Bobbin, Sardelic and I walked up the stairs to enter the court for the hearing, Syd's lawyers came over to us. One of them then pulled out a bundle of papers from a black briefcase and waved it like a white flag while another spoke:

'Let's talk about a settlement.'

'OK, we're listening.'

'Let's all just cover our own legal costs in this, and you are free to walk away.'

I looked over to Bobbin and he gave me one of his discreet nods and a hardly noticeable smile.

'OK, where do I sign?'

Halle-fucking-lujah! This was a great win for us; I'd just got my life back and was clear to go.

Could we have been awarded damages? Probably yes, because in a case like this the court usually ruled in favour of the employee. But pursuing damages would have meant I missed out on the America's Cup and *OneWorld*'s offer, so I let it drop.

Thus, after a legal fight and the longest six months of my life, I was now a free man.

When we walked from the court the warm Sydney sun had never felt so good on my freckled face. I stood there shaking hands with my legal team, patting them on the back and hugging my father. An enormous emotional and financial burden had been lifted from my shoulders. To this day, when I think back to what happened and why, the hairs still stand up on the back of my neck.

Now, the big question remaining was: would *OneWorld* still want me? After all, the only agreement that existed was a few words Gilly and I had scribbled on to the back of a napkin six months earlier. Obviously, I hadn't been able to formalise the agreement until the legal case was done and dusted. My overriding concern was that Gilly and his team might have been thinking that a sailor who had gone to court over an employment contract might be a problem within their own syndicate. I was anxious they might be thinking: 'What if this guy sues us now? Is he keen and for real? Maybe it is easier for us to look at someone else?'

Right then, my future held no guarantees and that was a worrying position to be in. I needed to know the answer as soon as possible, so I pulled out my phone and punched in the nine digits that would take me to Gilly's cell phone.

'G'day mate, it's Jimmy Spithill here.'

'Hey Jimmy, how are you?'

'Fantastic – I am ready to sign. Do you guys still want me?

'You bet! That's fantastic news. Let's meet tomorrow and get the ball rolling.'

A few days later, in February 2001, I signed a two-year contract with *OneWorld* and within weeks was in the wonderful position where I could pay back the money to my parents. Also, for the first time since I gave away my life savings of $5,000 to pay for the wrecked jeep, my bank balance was on the plus side of the ledger. I was no longer living hand to mouth.

On 21 February 2001, just days before the deadline for the America's Cup residency requirement, I had my passport stamped with a US visa in my hand. I went home, packed my bags, said farewell to the family and headed for the airport. I was leaving Australia permanently. Since then I have lived in America, New Zealand, Spain and Bermuda, but I still retain a soft spot for Australia.

As I flew out of Sydney, bound for Los Angeles, my mind turned back to Syd. He taught me a lot about sailing, legal issues and life. He believed in me and had the desire to give me a chance. Also, despite my young age, he put me to the test by giving me a great degree of responsibility. He blew up quite often, but I quickly learned how to deal with that. Instead of reacting I said to myself, 'Right-oh. Have your say, Syd. It's water off a duck's back for me.' Then I would get on with whatever I was doing. I hold no grudges towards Syd. We're mates again now. He did a lot for me and I still listen to him. I am for ever grateful for the chance he gave me – he believed in me and gave me one hell of an opportunity with *Young Australia* … he opened the door to the America's Cup! But I must say he made sure I had to kick that door off its freakin' hinges to get through it!

Despite the old boat and the lack of a shore crew and a proper base, alongside little financial support, the *Young Australia* campaign was the most fun. Why? Because there were no expectations apart from the ones we put on ourselves; we were just kids living the dream.

California Girl

The sensation that came with winning the court case against Syd was not dissimilar to how I felt when I walked away battered and bruised after that fight with the popular kid in primary school. However, there was one significant difference this time: I had not only stood up to the challenge without running away, I had won.

The immediate benefit from signing with the *OneWorld* team in 2001 was that I was now able to get a few perks ... like being able to book non-stop flights, and sleep in hotel rooms instead of on airport floors. Not surprisingly, as the jet climbed up and away to the east from Sydney, my mind rewound to when the boys and I started as a bunch of youngsters on the International Match Racing Circuit. It was certainly different now. Most importantly, though, the biggest bonus was that I could provide for my family.

While a nationality rule applied to the 2003 America's Cup, it was a bit of a lame duck. A lot of the sailors and shore crew on the Cup circuit were Aussies or Kiwis, and they all did what I had done to be able to compete: become a national of the country under whose flag the syndicate was racing.

Four other guys from *Young Australia* who had also signed with *OneWorld* joined me at the team's headquarters on the harbour in Seattle. As soon as we arrived, we felt as though we had won the lottery – we had gone from rags to riches. Initially, we were provided with an apartment, opened bank accounts and were each given a rental car. More benefits would soon follow.

We were given apartments in a trendy area called Kirkland, on beautiful Lake Washington.

There was not much for the team to do when we arrived in Seattle. It was early days, but we needed to be there to establish residency. To keep ourselves busy, we had physical training scheduled each morning. After that, I'd often hop into my car and drive up to Seattle's snow-capped backdrop, Tiger Mountain, to go skiing or hiking in the afternoon. On many of the days when I went there I was tailed by Joey, Bull and Andy, driving their matching Ford Mustang rentals and equally eager to shred the perfect spring snow. Whenever we wanted a bigger mountain challenge we headed for Whistler, which was only a four-hour drive away. Yes, I did pinch myself more than once...

Kirkland was a city of college students, so we fitted into the scene very nicely. At times our broad Australian accents made it difficult to order a coffee or a hamburger because we weren't understood, but it worked wonders when it came to striking up a conversation with some of the friendly locals.

The *OneWorld* syndicate also funded us to do the International Match Racing Circuit, the reason being that it was the best way to hone our skills in preparation for the one-on-one America's Cup-style racing. This time, though, there were some big differences for us as we prepared for the racing: being part of a Cup syndicate meant we were fully funded, and instead of hoping we would get a wild-card entry so we could compete, we were on the priority invitation list.

We made our mark from the start of the circuit with good results, and that meant more invitations to compete. We won numerous events and had a great year. Of all the events, our favourite was the one in Sweden, but not just because of the racing. We were in our element sailing and socialising, the latter made possible by the fact that the sun barely sets during summer. This meant many Swedes stayed up all night to party ... and we made sure we were part of that scene as well!

After we completed this circuit we knew it was time to get serious, and we did. In no time our sailing had gone from being plain fun to one of complete dedication, all because we wanted to win, and were expected to win. The pressure was on.

When the match-racing group and I arrived at the *OneWorld* base in Auckland in mid-2002, the rest of the sailing team was there and already training hard. It was an interesting experience for those of us who had been part of the *Young Australia* campaign. We couldn't help but compare our old life with the new. The syndicate, backed by tech billionaire Craig McCaw, wanted for nothing. We were staying in flash five-star waterfront hotel apartments near the Viaduct and had access to an array of resources to develop the AC boats. The boys and I were continually saying, 'Man, have we landed on our feet here?' The only thing missing were the European exchange students at the university campus from those *Young Australia* days.

Every morning started in the gym and was followed by breakfast. Next came a full day of sailing, then it was back to the base, unload the boats, have a debriefing and do a bit more gym work before returning to our hotel rooms.

On a personal front, my Sydney-based girlfriend Jorja and I were trying to keep our long-distance romance alive, but as anyone who has been in that situation will tell you, it's very difficult, especially at a young age. Inevitably, we both soon came to the same conclusion: 'Right now this is stupid, not enjoyable. Let's take a break and see where we go.' I have to admit it was tough to break up, but it turned out to be a blessing in disguise for both our lives and our careers. As fate would have it, Jorja went on to be a very successful musician in London, and I've become the professional America's Cup sailor I always wanted to be.

In October 2002, I couldn't help but notice a very interesting 23-year-old American girl who had just arrived in Auckland to be part of our *OneWorld* team. Everything about her was appealing – platinum-blonde hair, an ever-present smile, blue eyes and a Californian accent. She was always busy behind the scenes. She appeared to be putting in even more hours than I did – I'd see her in the office when I arrived for the crew training session just before 7am, and at night she'd often be the last to leave. Even so, her smile was always there. She was symbolic of our entire team: no one ever complained about their workload. This girl was impressive, to say the least. She reminded me of the times when my parents used to listen to the Beach Boys, in particular their iconic 'California Girls' – those guys sure were on to something!

This girl's name was Jennifer Wilson – Jenn for short – and she was employed as the team's environmental outreach coordinator. Needless to say, her presence made it even more of a joy for me to come to work every morning. This girl was an asset in every sense. What appealed to me immensely was that she was very natural. There was nothing fake about her – she's a pure, down-to-earth woman, a natural beauty inside and out.

On the sailing front we were flat out preparing and racing as hard as we could. Occasionally we would get a three-day break from training, and when we did, Bull, Joey, Andy and I would hit the town and meet up with some other team members at a pub in the Viaduct called the Bubble Bar. On one of these outings one of the team members to join us was Jenn... The moment I saw her I went straight to the bar and bought her a glass of champagne, thinking that's what she'd most want. 'Thanks very much, but do you think I could have a beer instead?' she responded. I almost proposed to her on the spot.

We started enjoying the beers, but then Joey lined up a round of shots and in no time we were throwing back these horrendous and potent drinks like there was no tomorrow. After downing quite a few of them, we confessed that we had liked each other from the moment we laid eyes on each other!

Those shots certainly broke the ice for us. I knew there and then that I'd met 'the one', and two years later Jenn and I married in Auckland.

* * *

During the first few months of the *OneWorld* campaign nobody – including me – thought I would be on the Cup race boat. My role was to be on the training boat and help push Gilly and his team to the limit, making sure they were well prepared for the Challenger Elimination series. Gilly had already explained it to me.

'Jimmy, we'll get you involved in the afterguard of the second boat. You can probably do a bit of grinding, maybe steer on the odd occasion.'

'That sounds great, Peter. I'll do whatever you want. I'd sweep the floor to be honest, I am so glad to be part of this team.'

However, as time went on, I was steering the second boat more often than not and when I did I managed to beat Gilly in quite a few of our internal match races. At that stage, no one imagined he would be doing anything but steer the race boat; he was the man. But then when I started beating him sailing the number-two boat, the rest of the team began to speak up, declaring that I should steer the race boat – let the results do the talking. That was it. I became the helmsman of the blue-hulled America's Cup race boat. I didn't let them down – we went through the first round of elimination races undefeated, one of only a few to take an AC race off legend Russell Coutts.

Everything was cruising along very sweetly for us as we prepared for the Cup ... until Craig McCaw, our principal financial supporter, lost millions overnight in the dot-com crash. That in itself was a lesson for me, and clearly reaffirmed why I don't like stock markets. I do have a lot of friends who play that game, but not me. I just don't understand why you would risk your money when so many variables over which you have no control can influence the outcome.

Anyway, the dot-com crash nearly put an end to *OneWorld* midway through the campaign. McCaw had gone from having millions of dollars' worth of stock one day to virtually zero the next. The money taps that had been gushing the week before were now barely dripping.

Luckily, the syndicate acquired another sponsor, Paul Allen of Microsoft, who was still able to fuel the campaign, but compared with before the crash our budget had become really tight. Unfortunately, the first thing to suffer was funding for our research and development programme. We were only halfway through the Cup challenge process and had no option but to abandon a number of design development projects we were working on. This would really hurt us because we could not develop and optimise the boat. Moreover, it wasn't just the research and development side that took a hit – the budget belt was tightened a notch or two across the board, including for all team members. We had to take a pay cut of around 20 per cent.

* * *

One day Jenn and I were invited to a house on Lake Tarawera, in the centre of New Zealand's North Island – the largest body of water among a string of magnificent lakes that surround one of the country's biggest volcanoes. This is where I met Aaron Toresen and his family. It was one of those classic situations where you immediately know you like the person; we hit it off from the outset and have remained great mates ever since. Aaron is one of those rare guys who pass the real tests of friendship. If ever I got into a serious bind or just needed help, he would stop whatever he was doing, jump on a plane and be there ready to join me in the trenches. I would do the same for him.

Like me, Aaron was also a boxer as a teenager – and became one of the best middleweights in New Zealand. Whenever possible, we would go on all sorts of adventures together – they were more like dares really, since we always pushed each other to the limit. There was the time when I decided to bring a bit of action to a party at the *OneWorld* base, jumping from the second floor of a building on to a marquee made from one of our strung-up mainsails. I slid down the sail and landed softly on my feet right in front of the ladies serving beer, an action that was seen as a bit of a James Bond moment. This prompted Aaron to try to match my effort but, unfortunately for him, he misjudged the jump, crashed off the marquee and finished up on his back on the ground alongside a group of surprised ladies who were enjoying their drinks.

We have great laughs whenever we go away together. He introduced me to hunting and trekking through the mountains in New Zealand. I was very sceptical at first because I'm an animal lover and wasn't sure I'd enjoy killing one. But after learning what it was all about, the level of respect and hard work, I now really enjoy it. We only ever shoot what we need, in a controlled and sustainable manner, and it's one of the most pure ways to put organic meat on your table and provide for your family.

* * *

Ultimately the *OneWorld* Challenge wasn't a successful one. We did make it into the final rounds, but then we were knocked out by *Oracle*, owned by billionaire Larry Ellison. Despite this, though, the campaign was incredibly valuable because it taught me and the others a lot about what you need to be successful in the America's Cup.

The fact was that being part of the *OneWorld* team proved to be a fantastic yet often frustrating experience. Why frustrating? With all the budgetary setbacks and time losses that came with the dot-com crash, we couldn't develop the boat anywhere near well enough. Even though it was well designed and built, it remained too conservative, and the winning boats were simply faster and ran better development programmes through to the end. The actual Cup match was dominated by the Swiss entry, *Alinghi*, which had Kiwi Sir Russell Coutts at the helm with his key guys alongside. It was his third consecutive America's Cup victory.

If the *Young Australia* campaign in 2000 launched me into the America's Cup stratosphere, then *OneWorld* in 2003 taught me how to lead a big team. *OneWorld* wasn't just any old team – in its ranks were several America's Cup winners who were older and much more experienced than I was. This experience proved to me that, given the right tools, I could lead a team and had the potential to compete against my childhood heroes and contemporary peers.

I truly felt I belonged in the America's Cup.

TEN

Parenthood

Often when I come home early to our yellow house on the north-central coast of Bermuda I am greeted by a sound reminiscent of slow tap-dancing. That's Jenn's knife dancing on the wooden board, chopping up whatever it is we are having for dinner. I am so fortunate that Jenn loves cooking and now has a degree as a nutritionist; my cooking skills are limited to burning the crap out of meat or fish on the barbeque – Australian for medium rare. Thank God Jenn is there because it means that our two boys, she and I are always eating the most nutritious food available. This is extremely important for me because of the training routine I face in the build-up to an America's Cup campaign.

Then, as I enter the front door, there's another sound I hear: little feet pattering across the marble floor. It used to be Owen, but now that he's nine years old, he is not as excited about me coming home as he used to be. But Joe, who is three years younger, is always excited if I get home before they go to bed.

'Daddy's home!'

'How are my best mates?'

It's sad but true that during the week I rarely see Owen and Joe. Most days they are still in bed when I leave, and already in bed when I get home. It's the one unfortunate aspect that comes with my role at Oracle Team USA. Still, I grab any chance that comes my way that allows me to get home before the boys go to bed.

In short, my role at Oracle is more than full time, and full on. Apart from the physical training and sailing, there are briefings to attend, ideas to discuss and develop with designers and the team in general, as well as all the commercial and promotional aspects associated with being the skipper of an America's Cup team. But I love it. I certainly wouldn't be happy doing a nine-to-five job.

For me, this entire programme has been, and will continue to be, an education process in itself. I've had the good fortune to be surrounded by people I look up to and respect, especially Larry, and from them I have learned that there is no luck in success: it only comes through hard work and dedication. It's difficult to explain, but I feel guilty unless I can look across at a competitor on the racecourse and know that I have done more than he has – that I'm better prepared than he is. I know I've probably been out of bed every morning while he's been asleep, and I'm still working towards my goal when he goes to bed. It's amazing how much 'luck' comes your way if you have this attitude.

Usually as a team we try to take one day off over the weekend. That's when I try my hardest to be a dad. We go swimming, fishing and boating, or I drive them to wherever they might be playing in a sporting competition.

Probably the most special moment when we are at home comes when I'm sitting in the living room and Joe runs towards me with his arms stretched out. I pick him up, swing him around, then he whispers into my ear.

'Can we wrestle, Dad?'

'Let's get it on, but we know I'm the champ.'

'No, I'm the champ!!!'

We both laugh, and soon Owen comes out of the boys' bedroom to join Joe and me for some rough and tumble on the living room floor. The warm buzz you get from hearing your children laughing happily is one of the few feelings that beat a perfect full-speed foiling tack when I am sailing. There's another highlight at the end of the day: I get to read them a story before bedtime.

I guess I'm now like any dad, really, but I used to think that I had an advantage over the family guys when I was single. From my perspective they couldn't train as hard as I could, or put the necessary time into a programme because they had to go home to a family. That caused me to think they were less motivated. But once Jenn and the kids became part of my life I realised that a family actually drives you to work even harder. Why? It's not just about you any more. Well, to a certain point it still is – but you are also doing it for someone else and there is more on the line. Moreover, after a tough day it is such a relief to come home to family who couldn't care less about sailing at that very moment. The children are so happy to see you, and they just want to get outside and wrestle or play. Now I actually think it is an advantage to have a family because it has really given me a more open mind, and I am even more motivated than I was before.

* * *

Rewind a few years to 2004. Jenn and I got married in one of the most beautiful places on Earth, Queenstown, New Zealand, right before summer kicked in. It was a stunning setting, with snow still capping the surrounding mountains.

We chose New Zealand because we both love this stunning country, and we wanted somewhere neutral. Having the wedding in the US or Australia would have made it really lopsided for one of our families. In addition, we figured it would keep the numbers down – but it didn't; a lot of friends and family still made the trek. I guess they used it as an excuse to come over for a holiday. Because of Queenstown's proximity to Australia, there were more Aussies, of course, but out of the 80 guests around 30 came all the way from the USA. We had a blast. The wedding was the curtain-raiser for three days of celebration – bungee jumping, jet boating, white-water rafting and sampling the produce from the local brewery. It was one of the best weeks imaginable. And with that 'yes' we all knew it was party time!

With the remnants of a hangover from the prolonged party still with us, Jenn and I snuck off to the Bay of Islands the next morning for a two-day honeymoon. I had chartered a big sport-fishing boat so we could do some hiking and cruising ... and maybe a spot of fishing.

Unfortunately, those two days were all the time I could spare before I had to head over to Italy and Spain to start working for the Prada-sponsored *Luna Rossa* America's Cup team. So, it goes without saying that I still owe Jenn a proper honeymoon – perhaps a land-bound one. Looking back on life, from the time I met Jenn through to when we were married and went on our honeymoon, it was all about boats. I proposed on a boat, spent my short honeymoon on a boat, made my living on a boat, and I spend a lot of my spare time on boats. That's caused me to think that being born with some toes that were webbed like a frog's was most definitely an omen.

Moving to Valencia, in Spain, for the campaign with the Prada team, for me meant diving in head first, but for Jenn it was a different story. We were thousands of miles away from family, in a new country with a different culture, and that meant she had to redefine her life and start from scratch. Luckily she honed her Spanish and became fluent over the couple of years we lived there, and she started an environmental non-profit organisation called Agua Limpia with a few of the partners of other Prada team members. She was able to find a purpose and do something she loved in a different country – something I admire. She didn't use 'being out of her comfort zone' as an excuse to sit at home and feel sorry for herself. This type of resilience and adaptability has become even more apparent over the years as each new campaign has meant another change of location. Having a partner who is flexible and up for new adventures has definitely helped me to do my job well.

* * *

Owen was born on 25 November 2007 at one of the best hospitals in San Diego, California. It was fortunate Jenn was on home turf for the birth for a number of reasons, not least the fact that the birth was an extremely tough process that resulted in her having a C-section. I was expecting it to be a gentle procedure, but in reality it involved a petite female obstetrician seemingly using all her strength to pull the baby out. I was in shock! I thought she was being overly rough so I told her to take it easy – but as I did so, out popped Owen, kicking and screaming. A real redhead! In a matter of moments I had this little thing cradled in my arms. It was as exciting as it was amazing. Simultaneously I realised nothing would ever be the same again.

We stayed in the hospital for four days, while Owen remained in the neonatal intensive care unit. A few days after we'd brought Owen home, I was on a flight out to Las Vegas to watch a classic fight at the MGM Grand Garden Arena: the bout between Floyd Mayweather and Ricky Hatton, who were both undefeated. Not ideal timing, but I had planned it with Aaron, who had flown over from New Zealand especially for what was billed as the fight of the century.

It turned out to be a great fight, and it seemed everyone was there to watch: Wesley Snipes, Will Ferrell, Bruce Willis, Brangelina, Gwen Stefani, Jude Law, David Beckham, you name it. In the first few rounds Hatton was able to put constant pressure on Mayweather, but in the 10th round Mayweather turned things his way and knocked Hatton down twice, both times with his explosive left hook.

As a father of young children, I now understand why my old man was dead against computer games. He relented eventually and allowed Mum to buy us a Sega Master System when I was in my early teens, but it didn't take me long to see why he didn't like them. There we were, surrounded by beautiful bushland and bays, and all we wanted to do was sit inside our little shack and play stupid games on a shitty old black-and-white TV. Fortunately, the novelty wore off after a few months, we weaned ourselves off it and then it suddenly disappeared. It got 'lost' as the old man put it. All I can say is 'Thank God!'

A lot of people get stuck for much of their lives in front of the TV screen. Yes, gaming does have a positive side: some gamers have amazing eye-hand coordination and are capable of making multiple decisions at a very rapid rate. But... I have followed my father's lead. Jenn and I have decided that our kids don't need any of that stuff. I think the outdoors and beautiful natural environment in which we live provides a far more exciting and healthy adventure for kids. Studies have shown that if children aren't brought up with some sort of social activity – a team sport or the like, in which you work as part of a group – they can struggle later in life because of an inability to interact through social contact. The idea that children will fall behind if they are not capable of using all sorts of electronic devices at a very young age is, in my opinion, complete bullshit. Computer skills can be honed at any stage in life, but it is far more difficult to learn how to socialise as you get older.

When we were in San Francisco with the Oracle America's Cup campaign, we enrolled our boys at the same school as the children of many senior executives of dot-com and tech companies. It is known as a Waldorf School and, incredibly, it was anti-technology. Naturally, Jenn and I thought it was ironic that parents who worked in tech would send their kids to such a place; one that doesn't allow technology in the school and recommends that you strictly limit all technology at home – including a ban on TV. However, it turned out that the reason many of these parents chose this form of education was no different from the one that prompted us to limit our children's access to computer technology and television. The philosophy is grounded in the belief that children need the opportunity to fully develop their social, imaginative, intellectual, and creative selves without interference from outside media sources. We have found through our own experiences that media can be counterproductive to imagination – and sometimes quite negative!

It all made sense, the one exception being watching sport on TV, something the boys and I like doing together – especially when Australia is playing New Zealand...

Learning from *Luna Rossa*

We swept down on Kiwi Chris Dickson like an eagle on to a mouse. From the word 'go' of the pre-start manoeuvring in the fifth semi-final of Valencia's America's Cup 2007 series, I dug my maritime claws deep into him and simply refused to let go. I wanted to embarrass him, and I knew I could. I was skippering *Luna Rossa*, the beautiful black Prada-sponsored boat with its emblematic red stripe, while Dickson was at the wheel of *BMW Oracle*.

The pre-start of a race is almost always critical to the outcome. When the five-minute countdown horns blast, both boats enter the starting area like bulls charging into an arena. This area is directly downwind from the start line, and you come in from the opposite side to your opponent. As it was our turn to enter from the starboard side, we had right of way over *BMW Oracle*, so it was easy for me to line Dickson up, by which I mean sail straight towards him and force him to turn his yacht directly into the wind, so I could match him. Then, with the two boats side by side and their sails flapping, we started trying to outmanoeuvre each other while sailing backwards, counting down the seconds until the start gun sounded.

Called a dial-up, this is one of hundreds of moves you can make against your opponent in a one-on-one match race, and on this occasion there was a good reason why we chose to execute it: I knew Dickson hated it. He performs much better when he can move his boat around but he couldn't do that this time. He was like a boxer trapped on the ropes. The crew and I aboard *Luna Rossa* had been practising the dial-up countless times during training and, as hoped, we had Dickson in a steady grip even before the start. Then came my psychological ploy: I looked over and smiled at him and kept staring him down. But it wasn't just about psyching him out; all the time I was watching his hands on the wheel, looking for the tiniest movement, one that would indicate the direction he would turn the boat in a bid to escape our hold over him.

The aggression I showed when sailing as a kid has become a tool of trade for me in the sport. I always wanted to hammer my opponents from the outset, forcing them to make a bad start by either being in the superior position when the start gun sounded or having a pre-start penalty imposed on the opposition for a rule infringement. With *Luna Rossa* this was somehow a must; our boat was much slower than *BMW Oracle*, so our only chance to win was to force our opponents into making mistakes or bad starts.

A good start is not rocket science – just like in chess, it involves a whole lot of moves and countermoves combined with instinct, as well as fantastic crew work and boat handling. You have to think ahead of your opponent, because then you can do something that the other guy won't expect. And just like in chess, there are no secret moves. It is all about being able to think five or even ten steps ahead and create unexpected combinations. And sometimes you have to make an instinctive decision with no time to think.

It's funny, I don't play chess – I don't have the patience for it – yet for my own game, which is like playing chess on the water, I can be out practising for days on end.

To master it I had invaluable help from Philippe Presti, who had spent hours and hours watching video recordings of Dickson sailing his yacht so he could analyse his tactics and moves. This enabled us to rehearse different manoeuvres and play out different scenarios so we would be ready to counter his actions.

Eventually I felt like I knew Chris Dickson better than he knew himself. It was also a given that I should try to take advantage of his well-known weakness – his temper. In a sense I was on a personal vendetta, because I believed that he had deliberately crashed into us in a pre-Cup event. I wanted to make him pay. Some people might see this as a shortcoming in my character – I never forget when people do wrong to my mates or me.

I knew Dickson wouldn't want to stay locked in alongside us and consequently I could see him getting more agitated by the moment. With a few minutes to go before the start, he made his move to escape but we matched him. He sailed off in the hope he could quickly turn *BMW Oracle* and come back at us when holding right-of-way, but we were ready for him. We attacked before he had time to make that move and forced him into an embarrassing position: he had fallen into his own trap and was subsequently given a red flag by the umpires for not giving way to us. Penalty number one – I was already having a good day in the office!

Even so, I had no intention of letting him off the hook to escape the additional pain I was planning to inflict on him. Both boats turned towards the starting line and again finished up side by side, with *Luna Rossa* holding a position that meant we had to stay clear of *BMW Oracle*. But then Dickson made a mistake. I guess my persistent presence was irritating him so much that he just wanted to get away, so he moved *BMW Oracle's* wheel as though he was spinning the wheel of fortune, but this time there was no fortune to be won. He turned his yacht into a downwind path, but in doing so slammed *BMW Oracle's* stern into our starboard side. Blue flag – second penalty for *BMW Oracle*!

'Humiliato!'

That was the spontaneous comment from the excited Italian TV commentators – and it said it all! For me, the noise of *BMW Oracle* whacking into our boat was like the clash of cymbals at the peak of a crescendo. Technically, I could have nailed him with a third penalty because he gained an advantage out of the collision – he was able to manoeuvre his yacht into a favourable position over us. That should have seen *BMW Oracle* black-flagged by the umpires and disqualified from the race there and then. Instead, they ignored it. Not that we were overly worried – we were able to sail away from the start with a huge advantage over *BMW Oracle*, which, when we looked back, was almost dead in the water while Dickson steered it through the penalty turns the umpires required the yacht to complete to erase the penalties. That race was ours from the start.

Historically, that was my best ever start. Cup experts also noted that never in the 156-year history of the America's Cup had there been such an uncompromising and forceful application of the rules to gain a pre-start advantage. America's Cup racing would never be the same again.

Our hostile approach to starting certainly gave the media something new to report that night, and it also provided our Italian fans with an unprecedented level of excitement, so much so that by the next day I had a nickname – Pitbull!

The following day Dickson, the man who was then one of the highest-paid sailors in the world, was taken off the boat and replaced by back-up helmsman Sten Mohr, but at that stage it was too late and we won our last race of the semi-finals to move through to the Louis Vuitton final against *Team New Zealand*.

Unfortunately for us, *Luna Rossa* wasn't on the pace, and we were no match for the Kiwis who made a clean sweep of us on their way to face *Alinghi* in the match. So after three years of campaigning we left Valencia empty-handed but with a lot more knowledge. However, as we would soon learn, much of it was knowledge that would not be needed for the next America's Cup match. 2007 was the last time that monohull yachts would contest the Auld Mug. The America's Cup was destined to be launched into an exciting new dimension in sailing – high-speed multihulls.

* * *

The *Luna Rossa* adventure had started immediately after the *OneWorld* campaign, when Francesco de Angelis, their skipper, reached out in search of a team. He flew both American high-performance sailor Charlie McKee and me over to Milan, where a black limousine picked us up from Milan–Malpensa Airport and drove us to a very clean and simple office. Inside, Francesco was waiting for us with Patrizio Bertelli, Prada's owner. Even though Bertelli didn't really speak much English, I got a good vibe from him from the word go. His interpreter was certainly saying the right things. I quickly realised that Bertelli was extremely passionate and knowledgeable about sailing and the America's Cup and I left the meeting thinking 'this could work'. Unfortunately, however, while it all sounded good, when it came to putting it into practice, it just didn't.

Regardless, I learned a lot.

Working in an all-Italian team while living in Spain was quite a cultural challenge after the *OneWorld* campaign mentality in New Zealand, which Joey, Andy, Ben and I were accustomed to. Even so, it felt as though we were in a family atmosphere with our teammates. When we had big get-togethers at the *Luna Rossa* base, with our families, it would be Bertelli with the tongs at the barbecue cooking the meat for the entire duration, refusing to move until he had provided for everyone. He really cared for his staff, and cooking for them was a way he could show that. Nothing was a problem for him. For instance, one time he used his private jet to fly in the meat we needed for one of our barbecues. The Italian family atmosphere was something special, but there were times when emotions would overflow; the highs after a good race were amazing, but in the tough times it would feel like a funeral.

Since we worked so hard wherever we lived, we didn't get out as much to enjoy the surroundings as we would have liked. That said, we did make time to enjoy some of the perks of a Mediterranean lifestyle, including kiteboarding, fantastic food and being able to pop over to the Balearic Islands for the weekend.

I know a lot of people struggled living in Valencia, Spain, but personally I really enjoyed it. It's a real family-based culture and I found the locals very friendly and hospitable.

In terms of the campaign we struggled with our technology and design tools. In any America's Cup it's about using sophisticated modelling software and design prediction programs – and back then wind-tunnel and tank testing for the hulls, masts and sails. Ultimately the biggest difference was that the boat was too heavy and lacked righting moment against the other teams in the semi-finals.

From a racing perspective I had one of my best years during this campaign. I sailed with Michele Ivaldi, Joey, Bull, Andy and Magnus: we wrapped up a World Championship as well as Grade 1 wins; and then with Jonathan and Charlie McKee, Manny Modena and young Mac Agnese: we were able to win the Melges 24 World Championship and a number of lead-up regattas.

Through taking on a lot of risk – aggressive sailing is not easy – we had managed to beat *BMW Oracle*, which was a much faster boat than *Luna Rossa*. But then we got absolutely smashed by *Emirates Team New Zealand*, skippered in the finals by Dean Barker; we didn't win a single race. I was bitterly disappointed with myself. I felt that I had let down the team by not being able to dominate the Kiwis on the start line like we had with *BMW Oracle*.

Still, in the end *Luna Rossa* brought me another rung closer to my goal of one day winning the America's Cup. I was taking it step by step and I knew I had to be patient. I had entered the America's Cup scene with *Young Australia* and had beaten one other team; then, in the next Cup match, I got to the Challengers Series semi-finals with *OneWorld*. Now, with *Luna Rossa*, we had made it to the Challengers Series finals. There was only one level to go for me – to challenge the defender of the America's Cup.

Dogzilla

'I think it would be really good if you came on board with the BMW
Oracle *team. Larry Ellison and I are putting together a new kind of
challenge and we will be building the team from scratch.'*

'Yeah, I would love to come on board and be a back-up for you.'

'No, no. I would be hiring you to hopefully helm the boat.'

I was pinching myself. Russell Coutts, one of the greatest sailors
in the world, who had now been hired by Larry Ellison to run the
American team, was proposing that I might have an opportunity to
helm his boat. Was this for real?

*'There are a lot of sailors out there, but there are very few who can do
everything. You have definitely developed as a racer; you have impressive
sailing abilities. You are not a leader yet, but you could be – if you want.
Do you want to be the complete package?'*

I didn't know how to answer, so I decided to shut up and listen.
Russell was on a roll.

*'We want to build a sailor-run team with a real collaboration between
sailors and designers.'*

Then came more exciting news: the other guys he was about to sign
would make this an America's Cup dream team.
  The essential ingredients for a team are real talent and being
a team player. What I have found interesting is that many high-
profile Olympic sailors have struggled to fit into the dynamics of

a large team – although the best of them always fit in. Conversely, sometimes the most talented, perhaps lower-profile, sailors are easy to miss. Now, by creating sailing's answer to Little League Baseball or college football with the introduction of the Red Bull Youth America's Cup, they are easier to spot. It is important for me and everyone else directly involved in the America's Cup to show kids that the sport requires athletes, it is cool and, most importantly, it provides long-term opportunities for them. Fortunately I have two 'experts' to advise me … Owen and Joe!

During the lead-up to the 2010 America's Cup campaign, the Cup went through a tough spot where there was more action in New York courtrooms than on the water. It wasn't the first time the America's Cup as a contest had been debated in court by rival syndicates.

The America's Cup is a charitable trust, to a large extent based on documents from the mid-19th century that were written when the owners of the yacht that first won the trophy in 1851 bequeathed it to the New York Yacht Club. The donation was made under a Deed of Gift, which stated that the Auld Mug was to be 'a perpetual challenge cup for friendly competition between nations'.

The Deed states that the winner of the America's Cup, and thus the defender of the next campaign, must appoint what is titled a Challenger of Record, a yacht club that will represent the interests of all the challengers and negotiate the terms for the next Cup match with the Cup defender.

To cut a long story short, and without diving too deeply into the complex legal technicalities, the Swiss team, Alinghi, had appointed a false Challenger of Record. Under the rules, the Challenger of Record must be an established yacht club that has at least already staged some yachting events; you can't just say as defender: 'I have a yacht club as Challenger of Record' when that club doesn't meet the criteria … and that is why Larry Ellison challenged the *Alinghi* syndicate in court.

The court ruled in our favour and consequently, *Oracle*'s home club, Golden Gate Yacht Club in San Francisco, became the recognised Challenger of Record, but that didn't end the confrontation between challenger and defender. The case continued. What kind of boats were to be sailed? Which countries were eligible to compete? Where was it to be staged? For a while things were going from one extreme to another – there was even talk about Ras al-Khaimah, one of the Emirates on the Persian Gulf, being the venue for the match, but in the end logic prevailed: the America's Cup returned to Valencia for a so-called Deed of Gift Match between the defender, *Alinghi*, of La Société Nautique de Genève, and a single challenger, *BMW Oracle Racing* of Golden Gate Yacht Club.

The Deed of Gift Match was based on the old Deed of Gift as amended in 1887: 'Three races shall be sailed, and the winner of two of such races shall be entitled to the Cup … if of one mast, [the yacht] shall be not less than forty-four feet nor more than ninety feet on the load water-line.' Simply put, there were no restrictions. Ninety feet! The foundation for the match was simple: it would be an 'arms race' … who could build the fastest 90-footer? It was time to go to the extreme.

Oracle's brains' trust came together and pooled their ideas. The next thing you know, we're building a huge trimaran, the likes of which nobody had ever imagined – 90ft long by 90ft wide! But the 90ft overall length only applied to the main hull, so another 10ft was added to the length of the outside hulls of our boat. While the designers, engineers and boatbuilders tackled their issues, the sailing team was working out how to operate this giant: a nautical version of an F1 car – a leviathan that could achieve a mind-boggling 40 knots on water. But making the challenge far greater for us was the fact that we were a team comprising mainly monohull sailors, and we had little idea about how to sail it. There was only one solution: learn as you go. We hired French multihull expert Franck Cammas as a consultant and soon after Glenn Ashby as coach to help get us up to speed in the world of multihulls. The first mast designed and built for the boat was 40m (130ft) high, and wing-shaped with a soft sail on the back. It was a concept that came with an apology from the engineers:

'We're sorry… This is really big. We're worried about it.'

But, after trialling it, the sailors would not give the designers' fears any oxygen:

'Go bigger. It's not powerful enough.'

That prompted the designers to step outside conventional thinking, and consequently create a rig unlike anything ever seen before.

In short, they were effectively taking an aeroplane wing made from the most exotic of space-age materials and standing it vertically on the yacht's main hull. It was a concept that meant the mast would be a highly efficient and remarkably powerful shape for any wind strength and direction. There was virtually no drag element to it – it was all about power and efficiency.

Wing masts, with a soft sail attached, had been used in the past, but they were a long way from being the ultimate answer. However, the performance numbers coming from our concept were telling a remarkable story: with this rig we would be able to sail up to three times faster than the wind strength. It was a no-brainer!

Russell gave Larry a call.

'We need to build the wing, Larry.'

'OK, but if we go ahead and do this, what's plan B?'

'There's no plan B, Larry. It's plan A. That's it.'

Larry is rarely lost for words, but he was this time. There was a distinct period of silence before he spoke, and not surprisingly it was classic Larry. His words were to the point, and as always, confirmed his trust in the people working for him.

'OK, you better make sure plan A works, then.'

The following day Larry called me.

'What do you think, Jimmy? Shall we do this wing or not?'

'Yep, we've got to do it.'

'OK, let's do it.'

When I hung up, I could only think, 'Shit, I hope I'm right.' This would be a huge undertaking and require an enormous amount of energy and money.

▲ Getting on the handles early.

▲ After getting my first windsurfer at the age of five, I was off any chance I got.

▲ With Tom (aka Spare Parts). He still can't drive a boat without flipping.

Dad in the tinnie towing Katie and me to the mainland for a race. ▶

◀ Borrowing the Hobie from the guy in our boatshed.

▲ With Syd Fischer and the *Young Australia* crew in our hospitality lounge on the barge.

▼ Our wedding day in Queenstown, New Zealand, 2004.

▲ On *Luna Rossa*, leading *Oracle* during the semi-finals in Valencia, Spain. *(Carlo Borlenghi)*

▼ The 90ft trimaran, training off San Diego, California. *(Gilles Martin-Raget)*

◀ Pretty lonely up here… *(Guilain Grenier)*

▼ First start in the 33rd America's Cup, against Alinghi, 2010. *(Gilles Martin-Raget)*

▲ 33rd America's Cup post-race press conference with Larry Ellison and Russell Coutts.
(Jose Jordan/AFP/Getty Images)

Winning my first America's Cup with Russ and Larry, 2010. *(Manuel Queimadelos Alonso/Getty Images)* ▶

▼ Nosediving during the San Francisco America's Cup World Series, 2012. We would go on to win the double, winning the fleet and match racing, the only team to ever do this … twice. *(Guilain Grenier)*

▲ Completing the 'double': JK, Joey, Jono Macbeth, me and Dirk 'Cheese' de Ridder, 2012. *(Guilain Grenier)*

▼ Mick Kermarec and Kyle Langford hanging 70ft up in the air following the 72 capsize, 2012. *(Guilain Grenier)*

▲ Mother Nature unleashing a full ebb current on us in 2012 and teaching me a lesson I won't forget. We ended up 10 miles offshore. *(Guilain Grenier)*

▼ Being dragged off the coast of San Francisco through the Potato Patch … a long night. *(Guilain Grenier)*

▲ Two-boat training in San Francisco Bay, 2013. *(Reuters/Peter Andrews)*

▲ Pre-race pads with The Honey Badger before Race 19, San Francisco 2013. *(Angie Silvy)*

◀ On stage before a race with Owen and Joe. Joe's got the right idea! *(Giulia Caponnetto)*

▼ At a San Francisco press conference in 2013. I ended up becoming good mates with Dean. *(Justin Sullivan/Getty Images)*

SAN FRANCISCO 2013
34 AMERICA'S CUP

▲ Match point, Race 19, 2013. (Guilain Grenier)

▲ We did it! I'm pointing at Larry Ellison in our chase boat – and (out of the picture) he's pointing at me. (Justin Sullivan/Getty Images)

▲ Taking *USA 17* back to the base after winning the 34th America's Cup in San Francisco Bay, 2013. *(Guilain Grenier)*

◄ Lifting the Cup for the second time, with Mum trying to take it off me, San Francsiso 2013.

(Guilain Grenier)

▲ Nude shoot for ESPN, 2014 … what was I thinking?! *(Steven Lippman)*

▼ Heading south to Hobart on the mighty Comanche, 2015. *(Andrea Francolini)*

▲ With super-coach and great mate Philippe Presti, 2017. . .
(Gilles Martin-Raget)

◄ 2017: the last day, before the race, walking to the boat.
(Ricardo Pinto)

▼ Pushing it hard in Bermuda, 2017. (Javier Salinas)

▲ Having a difficult time staying in front of the Kiwis, 2017. *(Ricardo Pinto)*

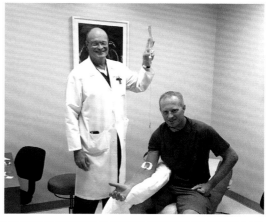

With surgeon and good friend Dr Rob Bray during our long series of intravenous injections. *(Layla Sotoodeh)* ▶

▼ Dr Bray and Dr Bulczynski saving my arm. *(DISC Sports & Spine Center/Garrett Bray)*

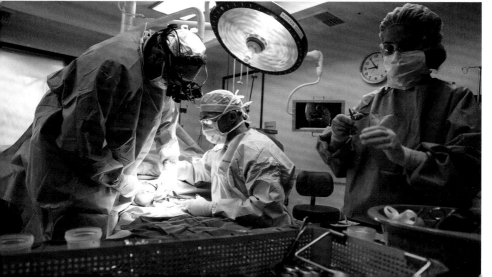

▲ Before completing (and surviving) a forward roll with Siegfried 'Blackie' Schwarz.

▼ Flying with the Blue Angels on an F/A-18 Hornet. *(Guilain Grenier)*

▲ Paddleboarding off the coast of San Francisco. *(Guilain Grenier)*

▲ Hunting and mountain climbing with good friends Aaron and Ben on New Zealand's South Island.

Dad, Katie, Tom, Mum and me, 2012. ▶

▲ Rock, Tom and a mate on his shoulder.

▲ Mum and Dad in 2015, moments before Dad launched his paraglider and flew down the valley.

▼ With Jenn and the boys in Lanai, Hawaii, 2013.

The team locked into the project virtually overnight, and in a very short time we had erased all the technical challenges, but we were still in the dark about how high the wing mast should stand.

I remember one of the early design meetings, in Paris, with French multihull design experts VPLP, discussing mast height. Initially it was based at 42m (138ft), which was by no means conservative. Then it grew to 50m (164ft), which prompted the comment: 'Wow, that's big.' But it didn't end there: we then went to 54m (177ft). The design process continued until a meeting at which one of the sailors mentioned a 60m (197ft) mast! I remember the same comment being made in one of the earlier meetings and the whole room erupting in laughter, like it was the dumbest thing somebody could have ever said. But no ... I was soon discussing a wing this size in fine detail with our design coordinator, Mike Drummond, in San Diego while testing the boat with the current conventional rig and we opted to go to the extreme: 69m (226ft) above the waterline. It would stand so high that you could not have sailed it under the Golden Gate Bridge!

Our challenger was to be named *USA 17*, but soon acquired a nickname from fans and press, *Dogzilla*, where 'Dog' is the abbreviation of Deed of Gift.

She would be propelled by one of the largest wings of any sort ever built by man.

THIRTEEN

Winning Our Way to the White House

Sailing *USA 17 – Dogzilla* as she was known to fans and media – was one of the most stressful experiences of my life, if not *the* most stressful. Because of the incredible power generated by the enormous rig, and the righting moment due to the weight and width of the platform, the load on every piece of equipment was colossal – to the point where I, and everyone else on board, had to constantly think about what was pointing at us, and whether we were in the firing line if it broke. During one training session, one of the pulleys – a traveller block – exploded, causing a solid metal pin to fly like an arrow through the air before embedding itself into a 2.5cm- (1in-) thick piece of carbon fibre at the bottom corner of the sail ... just 50cm (20in) above our heads. If it had hit anyone, it could have killed them.

Another threat was posed by the fact that the carbon-fibre bowsprit kept breaking off, again because of the enormous loads, and this meant that for months we didn't sail *Dogzilla* with the gennaker set on downwind legs. Not surprisingly, then, we were wondering from the outset if we were ever going to be able to tame this monster and get around a racecourse without incident. Everything about it was scary, but at the same time incredibly exciting.

During the period when the wing was being designed and built, we used the conventional carbon-fibre mast and soft sail for our training sessions. In reality, this was our 'Plan B' should the wing not live up to expectations ... which provided some slight relief for Larry, as well as for us. Hanging over our heads, though, was the constant realisation that no one had ever made a wing like ours for a sailboat, so there was no guarantee it would work until we tried it.

Much of the development of *Dogzilla* leading up to the Deed of Gift Match in 2010 took place in and around San Diego. On what started out as a Pacific postcard day, we took the opportunity to sail south towards Mexico, until everything went horribly wrong. We were trying a different sail combination but didn't have the load-sharing correct, to the point at which the conventional mast couldn't cope and suddenly snapped in two. The shockloads were such that some of the guys were thrown overboard, and Joey Newton would later tell me that he had chosen to roll off the boat and into the sea rather than wait for the mast to crash down on to him. Again, it was a pure fluke that no one was seriously injured.

However, as catastrophic as it was, there was an upside to this very dangerous situation – a classic example of how sometimes disaster provides the solution. This breakage left us in no doubt that we would not be racing for the America's Cup with a conventional soft sail rig – the wing was the way to go. We no longer had a choice; all our resources would go into the wing.

The adrenalin was pumping from that moment on. A vital decision had been made so we couldn't wait to experience the turbo boost that would come from such an efficient rig. But before that moment there were plenty of other problems that had to be confronted, such as how the hell would we get such a massive structure on to and off the boat? Time was of the essence, however, so we started to design and build the wing – charging ahead before we really understood how we were going to handle it.

Handling and logistics would always be a major headache. It required two massive hydraulic cranes to lift it up and get it on the boat, something we could only do when there was a favourable weather window, since any gust of wind could make it impossible to control – to the point where it could have been damaged beyond repair. It turned out to be a nightmare for all concerned every time we had to put it on or take it off the boat and we did, in fact, drop it on two occasions. The first was due to human error while it was being lifted off the boat using a crane, but the second time was a lot worse: it fell on to a concrete dock and was so badly damaged that we were unable to train for more than two weeks while it was being repaired. This was a costly experience in every sense.

The crew and I will never forget our first day of sailing *Dogzilla* using the wing – the reason being that we thought we had made an enormous mistake. But the problem was with us – we were trimming the wing to the wind angle as if we were sailing a conventional rig, and we were dead slow; nothing we tried made any difference. As we made our way back towards the shore my mind was running wild. Both Russell and I had convinced Larry that we needed the wing. Now millions of dollars had been spent and for what? Something that wasn't going to work.

When I got back to the dock, I walked towards our wing designers, Scott Ferguson and Joseph Ozane, who were waiting anxiously for our return, but my expression wasn't what they wanted to see. I was shaking my head in disappointment.

'Shit, guys, it isn't working anything like we expected. What have we done?'

It is one of the few times that I have seen these two guys visibly upset, but the more I explained everything that we were doing out on the water, the more their demeanour improved.

'Jimmy, you guys, you are doing this all wrong! We told you to sail off the instruments and the targets that we gave you. The wing isn't a sail – don't look up and trim it like you're sailing with a conventional rig!'

That evening, Joseph and Scott got the entire crew in the meeting room and went through a presentation on why we should trim to targets. When we went out the next day, we stuck to the settings they had given us, and instantly we were off! The lift coefficients we were seeing were almost beyond belief – two and a half times the wind speed! Suddenly the scary beast was working! Everyone on board was looking around in disbelief – and smiling, especially Dirk 'Cheese' de Ridder who was trimming it.

The best analogy for me to understand it all was to compare sailing that boat to flying an aeroplane. Pilots don't look out of the window to see what the wing is doing, they look at the instruments in the cockpit, never more so than at night or when they are flying through cloud. Those instruments give them the information they need to make adjustments when flying in constantly changing conditions, thus enabling the plane to fly at its optimum. So, when it came to *Dogzilla*, we had to re-educate ourselves to trust the instruments and balance out using our senses.

I was so intrigued by this new approach to sailing that I decided the only way to improve my understanding of the wing sail was to learn to fly. This proved to be an invaluable decision. The most memorable moment came when my flight instructor blindfolded me, then asked me to tell him which way we were flying. No problem, I thought. A few minutes later, when I was dead certain we were ascending, he told me to take off the blindfold.

'Holy shit!'

I nearly wet myself, because our little Cessna was heading straight for the ground as he pulled us out of a dive. Ever since that day I've trusted my instruments.

When I told the rest of the guys in the team about that experience, seat-of-the-pants sailing became a thing of the past; it was all instead about the numbers on the dials. In a very short time, we had two hulls clear of the water and were sailing at around 40 knots. *Dogzilla* – officially known as *Oracle USA 17* – was taking sailing where it had never been before, and that came with risks.

There were times out on the water, though, when we were confronted by danger that was not of our own making. On one of the last days of trialling off San Diego before shipping the boat to Valencia, for instance, we were romping along in perfect sailing conditions ... flying one hull and doing 38 knots. All of a sudden a giant black silhouette passed underneath us – a huge whale. We missed it only by inches. It was probably because our boat was so fast and efficient through the water that the whale didn't hear us coming, but it certainly knew we were there when we passed right over the top of it. There's no doubt about it, had the world's most powerful sailing boat collided with one of the world's biggest mammals, the boat would have been destroyed.

Damaging any major part of the boat was our greatest fear because, given that it was so complex and extreme, it would have been impossible to build a replacement in time for the Cup match. Still, if we were to have any hope in that contest, we had to sail it to the limit and maintain it with great vigilance.

In San Diego and in the early stages in Valencia, we thus removed the wing from the boat when weather allowed and stored it flat on trestles inside a canvas hangar on shore. This wasn't always enough, though. One night in Valencia, we were hit by a fierce hurricane with 60-knot winds that started tearing apart the canvas hangar. It was as if the weather had an insatiable appetite for the wing, and in return the wing seemed to like the attention: it was as if it wanted to join the party, doing its best to dance up and down each time a gust hit. For a while it was touch and go whether the wing would launch itself into the stratosphere. If that had happened, everyone around the harbour would have been ducking for cover because the wing would have exploded into pieces. In pure desperation, a number of us rushed into the tent and started punching holes through the wing and tying it even more securely to heavy blocks on the ground, which just about worked. It was a crazy time, and we were very lucky. We had steel superstructure falling from the ceiling; some team members refused to come in and help, it was so frightening. Had that hurricane had its way and trashed the wing, it would have been the end of our campaign.

Wind was an issue out at sea, too. When a conventionally rigged sailboat is about to be hit by strong winds, you can just pull down the sail, but with this thing there was no way of getting rid of it once it was up. Even if you had the boat at the dock, if it was windy there was no way the wing was coming out.

We all knew that everything about *Dogzilla* was dangerous and extreme – but if we were going to win the America's Cup in what would be an unconventional match at the time, we had to go to the extreme limits. I am still amazed that nobody got seriously hurt sailing that boat. The thing was so huge and had so much power; it was a freak of a boat, the like of which will probably never be seen again.

On the flip side, when everything was happening as it should and *Dogzilla* was locked in, the experience was pure ecstasy – incredibly fast, frighteningly powerful and amazingly smooth.

Unfortunately, though, those ecstatic moments were few and far between and too many times it scared the shit out of us. It was so fast that often the chase boats couldn't keep up with us.

In order to win the America's Cup we had to ensure that everything about the boat and the campaign was at its optimum. Accordingly, most of the time on the water was spent finding ways to better handle the boat and sail it faster. Then, when it was back at base, the shore crew spent endless hours doing repairs, adjusting systems and generally trying to make it bulletproof.

The Deed of Gift Match was to take place in February 2010, which is winter in Valencia. This meant that the weather would make things difficult for us since the winds were predominantly light, on average less than 8 knots.

Alinghi, of course, knew this too. Their Cup defender was a conventional catamaran with a conventional mast, and it appeared likely it would be a fantastic vessel for the expected light winds. Our trimaran could generate a lot of power in its rig, but we were of the firm belief that we would need winds of more than 8 knots for the boat to be at its best.

Sometimes, though, you have to be careful what you wish for. Spanish winters can deliver dramatic changes in weather patterns at very short notice, and never was this more evident than another horrible night in Valencia when conditions suddenly turned really sour. On this particular night, *Dogzilla* was attached to a mooring and our three-man night-watch team was on board to make sure the yacht remained safe, especially as the wing was in place. While we would have preferred to remove the wing at the end of each day's sailing, the procedure was so complex that it was deemed safer and much easier to leave it in situ.

Our watch captain, Magnus Clarke from Canada, had a protocol to follow should any problems arise, especially if the weather conditions deteriorated. These included a list of contacts he was to call depending on the threat to the boat, and if it became extreme and got to Code Red, he was to call me. It was about 2am when I was woken by the sound of my phone ringing. On seeing Magnus' name on the display panel, and simultaneously hearing gale-force winds hammering my bedroom windows, I realised there was trouble brewing. The alarm in his voice told me everything – he was highly agitated, even frightened. As he shouted into the phone, I could hear *Dogzilla* being tossed around so violently that the hulls were creaking and pounding in the background.

'We are in big trouble here, Jimmy; we can't keep her on the mooring ... she's going to destroy herself. We're gonna have to take her out of the harbour.'

'Don't fucking leave; I am grabbing the guys and we'll be there in a matter of minutes. Do not fucking leave.'

I knew that there was no way Magnus and those with him could navigate *Dogzilla* out of the harbour safely in such extreme conditions; frankly, in those conditions neither could we.

The moment I got to our base and leaped out of the car, I could see *Dogzilla* bucking like a wild bronco desperate to dislodge its rider. The boat was launching itself so high into the air then landing with such force that some of the ropes used to secure it to the mooring were snapping like pieces of string. Each time the hulls crashed back down to the water it sounded as though the boat was exploding. There was only one thing to do: get out to *Dogzilla* with new lines and do our best to restrain it before it broke up. We thus jumped into our inflatable boats and cautiously negotiated our way out to the yacht, but were reluctant to get alongside because it was pitching so dangerously. In reality, we had to somehow get men on board if we were going to save it. However, each time we got close enough we had to abandon that effort because there was every chance someone would be seriously injured.

Still, we persisted, and after countless attempts, a favourable wave pattern arrived on the scene and in those few seconds we were able to get men on board. Then, in what was an amazing combined effort between those in the inflatables and those on the yacht, we were able to set more anchors, hoping they would be enough to enable *Dogzilla* to ride out the storm. By morning, our determined effort was well rewarded. After what was a brutally long night, the storm abated and the yacht had survived.

* * *

The days leading up to the Cup races were worrying times. While we were confident our boat would be faster upwind, there was a question mark hanging over the downwind sailing; we thought there was every possibility *Alinghi* would have our measure. However, our biggest problem was that we were constantly breaking deck gear and fittings – a concern that we took into the first day of racing. Getting around the course without a major breakdown was as big a challenge for us as getting home first.

Strong winds kept delaying the race, which was disappointing to us as we believed our best chance would come when there was a solid breeze blowing, while *Alinghi* would be wanting next to no wind to show her best form.

Not surprisingly, then, the *Alinghi* team were doing everything they could to hold off the start as long as possible, a situation that made life very stressful for the crew and me since our boat was a real handful when cruising around and not racing in those conditions. All the while our boat was slamming into the waves, and with each slam the wing was creaking and making all sorts of unsettling noises.

The wait went on for hours and there was no opportunity for me to relax because I dared not hand over the helm to anyone else in case something went wrong. If I did hand over the helm, I knew I would have to take it back just minutes later, and I would have been so anxious I would not have been able to relax, and that would be more mentally exhausting than sticking with it. I knew from my labouring days and physical training that I had the stamina to work all day without taking a break, but it's very different when mental exhaustion comes into play. There was also a high level of anxiety in the air at this time because neither team knew which of the two boats would be faster.

Eventually the wind settled down to a steady 12 knots – a nice sailing breeze by most people's standards, but the *Alinghi* team declared they didn't want to race, claiming it was too windy and too rough with a 1–1.5m (3.3–4.9ft) swell running – I mean, come on! But eventually they were forced into it. The race was on. And there was one big surprise prior to the start when the defenders announced that the head of the *Alinghi* syndicate, Ernesto Bertarelli, would be steering the boat.

We decided to come out with all guns blazing for this first start, and it had the desired impact. They were shocked by the ferocity of our attack – they certainly didn't expect this level of aggression from a team sailing such a monster boat. In no time at all we had them cornered and before the race even started they had received a penalty from the umpires for not keeping clear of our boat.

Philippe and I had spoken about this start and the dial-up manoeuvre and he was really worried about it. The reason for this was that we had taken the main hull rudder off, as when we were straight-line sailing it wasn't needed. However, this made down-speed manoeuvring extremely difficult, as the rudders in the outside hulls were barely in the water when the main hull wasn't flying. Before we knew it, we found ourselves stuck in irons, and to add to that we had a primary-winch engagement issue and could not trim the jib on to get the boat from being dead in the water.

While this was happening, *Alinghi* got out of our control and started sailing up the first windward leg. After what seemed like an eternity the winch kicked in, and we took off across the start line. Once underway, we set off in pursuit of *Alinghi* and before long were pleased to realise we had a speed edge on them, primarily because we could sail our boat harder, and therefore faster, in those conditions.

Our big challenge was to make sure we never overloaded the boat. If we did, God knows what the consequences might be – structural failures or the rig going over the side were just two possibilities. During training, we had an alarm system in place comprising laptops and fibre-optic cabling attached to key areas of stress. Whenever things were overloaded, loud fire alarms went off – which was the majority of the time. But for the racing, we stepped into the future. Instead of the screens, all the relevant data was relayed to my sailing glasses, which had a heads-up display. I could see all the information inside my glasses, Terminator-style, and to save weight took the physical speakers off the alarms.

On that cold February day, I kept pushing the boat harder and harder, confident that the safety factors we had built into the boat were not being breached, even though the alarms were ringing like Christmas bells inside my sunglasses. We had to push as much as possible because there was no certainty that we would be faster than our opposition downwind. However, when we did turn on to the downwind leg, we had a nice surprise: *Alinghi* was slower than us, not faster! Victory was ours, and how sweet it was. We passed them and led them home by a huge margin – more than 3.5 kilometres (2.2 miles).

I still wasn't confident after this race, though – I was worried we were going to break something major. But the only way to have a chance at winning was to push it. The Deed of Gift Match was a best of three, so we only needed the boat to hold together for one more race for us to be able to raise the America's Cup above our heads.

The second race was sailed over a triangular course in light winds, and again things went in our favour. *Alinghi* gave itself a penalty in almost unbelievable circumstances. They were penalised for not being outside the starting zone when the five-minute signal was sounded – one of the most fundamental mistakes anyone can make in a match race.

This time we got away from the start with a good lead and sailed towards what we believed would be the favoured side of the course, while *Alinghi* – still carrying their penalty – went to the opposite side and got it right: they found stronger wind. However, once we were back in the breeze, we started to reel them in. By the time we reached the first mark, we had passed them and established a lead of 28 seconds. From that point on they had no answer: at the second mark our lead was 2 minutes 44 seconds. Again, the alarms were celebrating Christmas inside my glasses, but I didn't want to ease off the pace so I just kept pushing as hard as I dared while trying to balance the loads.

This was the craziest, most extreme America's Cup ever, and there will never be another one like it. In the end we triumphed. History shows that on 14 February 2010, team *BMW Oracle Racing* reached the third marker – the finishing line – and claimed the America's Cup for America. The winning margin was an amazing 5 minutes 26 seconds.

Our success established a record in the annals of the America's Cup: at 30 years of age, I had become the youngest winning skipper in the 159-year history of the event.

The dream of a little nine-year-old redhead had come true! It is hard to describe, but if you ever achieve what you have worked towards your whole life, it is almost too much to comprehend at that moment. I had finally got it done. I thought about everything I had been through: the campaigns, the personal battles, the struggles to succeed, and instantly I felt it had all been worth it. The triumph lifted a great weight off my shoulders. So much had been at stake, which is probably why it felt so rewarding – it had been *so* hard.

The best part for me as we crossed the finish line was seeing how excited all my teammates were, including Russell and especially Larry, who had finally won the America's Cup at his fourth attempt and was on board with us for the final race. The ride back from the finish line to our base in the port was just one of the coolest moments imaginable. We were all together on *Dogzilla* for 20 miles before hitting the dock, followed all the way by a huge fleet of spectator boats and a squadron of media choppers in the air, with Larry driving and pushing it the whole way.

Even before we hit the shores, armchair critics were speculating about the boat, some of them saying that anyone could sail that monster. Yeah, right. It is like saying anyone could ride a rodeo horse – and a 70m- (230ft-) tall rodeo horse at that. I know that we won for one reason only: we were the better team, with the better boat, simple as that.

As soon as we hit the shore, we had to get the wing down – an endeavour that proved as difficult as ever. I had to let the crew deal with much of this task since I had to go to the presentation of the America's Cup, which was to be handed over to Larry, Russell, John Kostecki and me. My most vivid memory of that ceremony was the amount of champagne that went through the air and just about drowned all of us.

It was wonderful to have Jenn and Owen there with me, and to see the trophy handed over in front of a huge crowd. The Spanish love fireworks, the noisier the better, and the display they put on was as awesome as it was frightening. (In fact it was too frightening for Owen, who was soon bawling his eyes out. For some reason this sticks in my head.)

The next day I got incredibly sick – not hung-over, but down with really bad flu, probably because there was no longer any stress on my body, so my immune system decided to take a holiday.

Over the ensuing months, we all struggled to comprehend the impact and extent of our success, but there was some indication of it when a message arrived from President Obama inviting the team to the White House. What an honour that was for all of us. Four months later, almost the entire team arrived at the White House for a presidential reception. The President was genuinely interested in what we had achieved, asking many questions about the boat, including the different loads that were exerted on the hulls and rig. As a thank-you gift to the President, Larry presented him with one of *Dogzilla's* steering wheels.

Heroes, Hunting and Nakedness

I grew up amid the amazing stories of the Australian and New Zealand Army Corps or ANZACs, as they are better known; riveting tales about the incredibly heroic deeds of the corp's soldiers in World War I and beyond. The history of the ANZACs goes back to 25 April 1915 when Australian and New Zealand soldiers were part of an allied force that set out to capture the Gallipoli peninsula in Turkey. The odds were grossly stacked against them, but the grit that these young blokes showed became the foundation of a legend that always stirs national pride.

These soldiers were real war heroes, and their stories make for enthralling reading. I thrive on them, and love books such as *Mark of the Lion* by Kenneth Sandford, which is the story of a Kiwi soldier, Charles Upham – the only man to receive the highest honour of all, the Victoria Cross, on two occasions during World War II. The stories of more recent heroes, such as US Navy SEALs Marcus Luttrell and good mate Matt Bissonnette (pen name Mark Owen), are also high on my list.

I think if there's a common link between them all, it is that they are great leaders. I am drawn to the team and brotherhood dynamic of the military, and the fact that it is always tough going. These guys will do anything for each other: they would literally jump on a grenade to save the others. That kind of relationship is extremely rare. In Australia we call it mateship.

I am so impressed by the fact that these men are doing something for others while getting little or no recognition for it. They are completely away from society's spotlight while making the ultimate sacrifice. Talk about letting the results do the talking!

I have been fortunate to meet ex and current SEALs in recent years, and what always stands out is how low key and unassuming they are. Yet they all have this aura and confidence about them.

I can imagine myself being in the military; it's one of my regrets that I didn't serve my country. To be honest, I feel I took the coward's option.

With all this in mind, I often wonder where I would be, and what I would be doing, if my professional sailing career hadn't taken off when I was 19. Fate is an intriguing master.

* * *

As I kneel down on one knee on the wet rock, I try to take control of my breath – even though we have been pounding around, up and down steep ravines for hours with heavy loads on our backs. I concentrate and manage to quickly get my pulse down. At that moment the deer, a red stag, comes into my rifle sights. I take another breath ever so slowly, then another, before I place my index finger on the trigger. At the same time I sense beads of sweat trickling down my spine.

As I mentioned earlier, it was Aaron who introduced me to hunting and taught me how to use a high-powered rifle. I have since grown to like guns – the engineering, their power, their accuracy, and the competition of trying to hit a target. For some time Aaron tried to coax me into going hunting with him, but he never forced the issue. I eventually agreed of my own volition to join him in New Zealand on a hunting trip. Still, I was apprehensive.

We were taken by helicopter to the middle of nowhere; a place where the landscape was straight out of *Lord of the Rings*. This scene became more remarkable about 10 minutes after we landed, when the noise of the departing chopper faded into the distance. Now it was just Aaron, our guide and good mate Brian Elwarth and me, all lugging backpacks that were crammed with everything we needed to survive for five days. And ... it was pissing down with rain, but I couldn't stop smiling.

When the weather cleared, I was in awe of the scenery around us: high ranges with craggy peaks covered in snow, deep ravines, lofty waterfalls with ribbons of white water pouring down their faces, and canyons enveloped by dense low clouds. The only thing missing was Bilbo Baggins running out from behind a rock. This was brutal yet beautiful hiking at its best. If there was a problem, it was that there were no hiking trails; it was as if we were trailblazing explorers going where no one had been before. But we had Brian, whose orienteering skills had us making our way safely and positively across an unfamiliar land.

After trekking for almost a day, Brian declared we were closing in on some deer, but there was no surge of excitement among us. Both he and Aaron are very selective when they go hunting; it's never a case of simply shooting the first animal you see. When we came across potential targets, Brian would take control:

'Nah, we're not taking that one – not old enough. Not that one either; she has little ones.'

Eventually Brian gave me a nod, indicating that the big red stag I had in my sights was there for the taking. He was about 200m (650ft) away and looking straight at me. Ever so gently I applied pressure to the trigger. Then came the amazing sound – CRACK! The noise of the shot was echoing through the mountains around us as I lowered the rifle and looked at my target. It was a perfect shot – a direct hit. The stag was dead within a split second. Having been an animal lover all my life, I had always wondered how I would feel in this situation, and my reaction actually surprised me. It felt OK. I was not overflowing with joy or adrenalin, it was more of a moment of respect. It's difficult to explain, but you share a special bond with an animal when you succeed in hunting.

Nothing from this stag was wasted. We carved it up and shared it around. I added 40kg (88lb) to my backpack – fresh meat for my family and friends. It doesn't come any more organic than that.

Over the years I have come to love hunting, simply to provide wild meat for our own table while enjoying the natural beauty that comes with being outdoors. Actually, I'm looking forward to introducing my boys to it, not simply to shoot an animal, but to appreciate the trekking, camping and other adventures involved. In today's world it's easy to take for granted how food gets to your table. On a personal front, I know that hunting and hiking help my sailing; they get me into another environment – away from a world of high technology and high intensity and back to the peace and serenity that only nature can provide with no distractions.

* * *

The period between winning the America's Cup in Valencia and defending it in San Francisco in 2013 gave us the chance to really change the game. With Larry and Russell leading the charge, we looked to the future of our sport and what needed to be done to make the Cup match appeal to a much wider audience. We came up with sailing's equivalent of Formula 1 race cars – large and incredibly fast hydrofoil catamarans; sailboats that lifted clear of the water and literally flew around the racecourse at unprecedented speeds. It was a concept that was far more TV and spectator friendly, as much a roadshow as a regatta. There was great emphasis on the sailors, the on-water and onshore atmosphere, and a style of racing that everyone could understand.

This focus led to some bizarre and completely unexpected moments for me, such as the time I received a phone call from an associate at Red Bull.

'Hi Jimmy. Have you heard of the ESPN Body Issue?'

'Yeahhh … well, kind of.'

'It's the sports channel's magazine, and every year they publish an issue where they photograph some of the best athletes in the world. No male sailor has ever been invited to participate – and they want you to be the first!'

'Sure. Why not?'

'Of course you know it's a nude shoot.'

'Excuse me?'

'Yep – in your birthday suit. You'll be great. I'll call them now and tell them you're in. Cheers, mate.'

A nude photo shoot is not something I would seek to do, but when I thought about it I realised it was a good opportunity to raise the profile of the sport and what we were doing with the America's Cup. At the time we were still dealing with the stereotypical image of fat, non-athletic skippers and sailors. I also accepted that the photo shoot would take me out of my comfort zone; it's not as though I am happy to run around naked in front of a lot of people. This was a challenge, and I love challenges. Decision made: 'Fuck it. Let's do it!'

I was already reasonably fit, but I wanted to look my best if I was going to be doing this for the sport, so I went to see our Oracle Team USA fitness coaches, 'Oscar' McFarlane and Brent Humphreys, and they established a two-week, get-toned-quick training regimen.

On the day of the shoot it was as if a circus had come to town – a huge entourage turned up! It included the head photographer – the famous Steve Lippman – his assistants, a lighting crew and a couple of others who were 'gophers' for anything that was needed. In total there were no fewer than 20 people – a mix of guys and girls. In addition, I had two mates with me: guys from the shore crew to drive a support boat and a camera boat. We did the shoot on San Francisco Bay on what was a gnarly, windy and bitingly cold day – not exactly ideal conditions for a nude shoot.

I must say I was happy knowing Lippman was the photographer, since he's recognised as 'one of the most explosive and diverse photographers around today'. Even so, I felt pretty uncomfortable when he said, with a casual air, 'OK dude, let's go. Take your gear off!'

I didn't reply. I just got on with it, taking off my board shorts then cupping my hands over my 'man bits' because I was feeling extremely self-conscious. However, after 20 minutes of photos being taken from a dozen different angles I just didn't give a shit, nor did anyone else. It was as if they were saying, 'Yep, there is Jimmy naked. Who cares?' The only problem for me was that by then I was shivering my butt off – the wind-chill factor made it almost unbearably cold. Perfect for a nude shoot... The good news is that despite the conditions the photos obviously turned out all right because they were published in the magazine.

FIFTEEN

Death and Destruction

2012 was the year of the revolution – the year when the America's Cup took the quantum leap that led to sailing becoming a full-on and exciting extreme sport.

It involved the introduction of high-speed hydrofoil catamarans, the likes of which had never been seen in the Cup's 161-year history. But, not surprisingly, this extreme change triggered a wave of resistance within the sport's hierarchy. Many pundits and sceptics were stridently opposed to it and some Cup aficionados from yesteryear were adamant it just wasn't sailing, and it certainly wasn't the America's Cup. However, once they saw the speeds these boats could achieve – well over twice that of a conventional America's Cup monohull – they began to come round.

Once the design parameters for these boats had been agreed upon, we set about planning the build of the first boat for Oracle Team USA. It was as challenging as it was exciting for all involved, since we were entering a world we knew very little about. The America's Cup class was to be 72ft long and feature a rigid two-element wing for a mainsail, as well as a conventional jib. It was to be sailed on the waters of the notorious San Francisco Bay.

The biggest change, though, was the addition of hydrofoils. Eventually only the foils and rudders would remain in the water when we were racing, meaning the cat would literally fly 1.5m (5ft) above the surface … and the crew were the pilots.

But while this was a formula for great excitement for the sailors and spectators, it also meant there was a much higher level of danger. The hulls were narrower and the bows considerably finer than those of a conventional catamaran, with the result that they would be prone to nosediving following the slightest mistake being made on board. The greatest contributing factor to this threat was the power generated by the 40m (131ft) carbon-fibre wing sail. It was unforgiving. When compared with the power of a conventional soft sail rig, the wing gives the boat a turbo boost of unimaginable proportions. We soon realised that on mastering the foiling, and with the wing at its most efficient angle to the wind, we could sail at up to three times the speed of the wind.

Our design represented completely new technology and broke all existing boundaries, even those of *Dogzilla*. Fortunately, we were able to apply some of the technology and features from that boat to our latest design, but even so, we and all other Cup teams were on a very steep learning curve.

Never was the danger involved with sailing these boats more evident to us than on Tuesday 16 October 2012. The forecast for San Francisco Bay for the day was what we were hoping for: a steady 15-knot wind, ideal for us to test our brand-new, week-old boat. But no sooner had we launched it and sailed away from the dock than – BANG! – a 20–24-knot westerly wind howled in from the Pacific and across the bay. Still, we weren't deterred because we had to push this boat to the limit in preparation for the Cup defence, which was just 10 months away. However, as we would discover on that ill-fated October day, we were nothing but L-platers – we had no fucking idea what we were doing. It was like going to the Moon back in 1969 … nobody had done it.

Don't ask me why, but the foils we were using at that early stage were nothing short of extreme. Even now, with all the training we've done since, I am not sure if we would be able to manage sailing with foils shaped like those.

What made them so crazy? There are a lot of physics involved, but in a nutshell: the more V-shaped the foils are, the more stability they provide, but they also deliver more drag, which slows you down. The more L-shaped they are, the faster they cut through the water, but at the price of stability. As we would soon learn, the foils we were using were mega-fast, but offered zero stability. Making matters worse, the rudders were much too short, and the rudder wings weren't big enough to provide fore-and-aft stability. We also hadn't realised that we needed to constantly trim and adjust the foils like a pilot would do with the ailerons on a plane wing. Instead, it was virtually a case of set-and-forget and, unbeknown to us, we had a formula for disaster on our hands. It was one that would lead to the mother of all capsizes simply because there were myriad problems unfolding that we had not anticipated.

Around noon that day, the last wisps of the famous San Francisco Bay fog lifted and revealed a clear blue sky. We were sailing laps around the bay, heading first towards Alcatraz Island, on to Treasure Island then down to the Golden Gate Bridge. Once there, we would bear away in the westerly wind and head back into the bay. It was always our intention to stay on the city side of the bridge because once you are beyond it, you are entering treacherous waters.

Every time we got close to the bridge the wind was stronger than that we had experienced on the previous lap, a fact that made the turn downwind – a bear away – more challenging each time. It's actually during a bear away that you are most prone to nosediving, so timing everything perfectly is critical.

As we headed past Alcatraz and towards the bridge, we were sailing at what seemed like warp speed. I turned to speak to Dirk 'Cheese' de Ridder, who was sitting next to me.

'Good breeze, eh? Looks pretty fresh.'

'We need to be careful here, Jimmy, it's getting fucking windy.'

I really should have seen it coming. During the afternoon the current had turned to be on the ebb, a current so strong it feels like it is going to drain the bay of all its water. When it is on the ebb and running against a strong westerly sea breeze it creates steep head-high crests, waves so large that I often surfed them on my paddleboard.

Just before 3pm, after getting back to the bottom of the bay and having survived a marginal bear away, I spoke to Cheese and Tom Slingsby about whether or not we should head back. This caused me to make a decision that would haunt me for months to come, and prove very costly.

'It looks like it has died down a bit. Let's do one more lap.'

'OK, Jimmy.'

Off we went towards the Golden Gate Bridge one more time, and pretty quickly we were in a lot of trouble because the wind hadn't died at all – it was actually getting stronger. Normally, when watching a video of sailing in rough conditions like those we were experiencing, the sea looks like a millpond, and I don't know why. But if you look at the YouTube video of us taken that day by an amateur cameraman on the bridge, it looks as though we were sailing through a hurricane – confirmation that the wind was so strong it would just about blow dogs off chains.

It was howling in at 28 knots when we had to commit to bearing away and turning back into the bay, and as we did so I remember wishing that sailboats had brakes. We were completely overpowered by the wing sail and there was nothing we could do about it. We were at full throttle and I had to make the call.

'OK. Let's go for it.'

We went for it all right. We angled the foils at 3 degrees, held on and put the hammer down, which was the only way to go. But it wasn't the only thing that went down.

When we started the turn we were in semi-foiling mode, but as we accelerated, my whole body told me that shit was about to hit the fan! We were doing about 40 knots when the lift from the foils caused the cat to leap out of the water, go bow down and spear into the water. It was a huge nosedive, like driving a car straight off a cliff!

All I could do as we went was scream out to the lads…

'Just keep an eye on your mates!'

Whenever we were out on this boat, we were always miked up through our helmets so we could communicate. The chatter was always constant, but in this situation things were so scary there was a deathly silence for quite a few seconds – the time it took for the cat to complete her 90-degree flip. We came to a stop when the bows were pointing at the seabed and the sterns at the sky, because the buoyancy of the wing mast had stopped us from cartwheeling and ending up upside down.

'Fuck, it's happened', was my first thought. But within a heartbeat a real sense of urgency kicked in: we had to get everyone off the capsized boat as quickly as possible.

The majority of the crew was still hanging on in the cockpits in the hulls, but the chatter through helmet mikes initially made us realise two were missing – Kyle Langford and Mick Kermarec – until we looked skywards. There they were, more than 10m (33ft) above us, clinging to the then vertical netting that stretched between the two hulls. Both of them were spreadeagled and looking like Spiderman.

If the situation hadn't been so serious that scene would have been funny. But all I could think was how lucky we were that the mast hadn't broken as the boat pitch-poled. If it had smashed to pieces as it hit the water then we would have flipped upside down and all of us would have been pinned underwater. I don't want to think about what the consequences might have been had this happened.

I then did a headcount that I thought confirmed everyone was still with, if not on, the boat. The chatter among the guys confirmed that Joey Newton had had a lucky escape. He was hanging on to the side of the cockpit after being washed overboard by a wave that hit when we were at maximum speed in the bear away. Fortunately, Rome Kirby had seen him go and was able to drag him back into the cockpit before he lost his grip.

The carbon cockpits weren't designed for it, but ours turned out to be a perfect little safety capsule. So, we were all tucked in, waiting for the grinding noise of the boat to come to a halt. We didn't want to jump into the water because there was a risk of debris falling on to our heads or of landing on razor-sharp foils and rudders. Once the boat was weirdly stabilised with half of the hulls buried underwater and the boat looking as if it was in the process of doing a headstand, I did another quick headcount, yelling to the guys to check if everyone was ok. Then, one by one, we started climbing down the 22m (72ft) tower to where we could jump into the water and swim to our chase boats, which had been following us. Because the boat was likely to break up, it was too dangerous for them to come alongside so we could jump on board.

The only option was for us to leap into the turbulent and cold grey water, and swim to the boats through the waves. I was the last guy to jump ship but it took me longer than I would have liked: one of our big winch-grinders had gone into shock and wasn't confident he could climb down and be rescued by the chase boats, so I decided to persuade him...

'Mate, if the wing breaks we will be pinned underneath and you will drown. Climb the fuck down NOW!'

My subtle persuasion worked: he immediately got going. That meant I could honour the maritime custom that the captain should always be the last to leave a sinking ship ... or so I thought.

As soon as I got to one of the chase boats I shouted to everyone:

'OK, let's do a proper headcount; make sure we've got everyone.'

As well as the 11 crew members that day, we had two additional sailors and one of the designers on board as observers – a common practice on training days.

Suddenly I realised we were missing one. 'Who the hell was missing?' I asked myself, while doing my best to stay calm. It's probably just confusion, I thought.

'Let's do a headcount again.'

'Shit, we are still missing one. Who's not here?'

Suddenly, it dawned on me.

'Murray! Where the fuck is Murray?'

Murray Jones, the legendary winner of five America's Cups, was nowhere to be found. Our rescue diver, South African hard man Jan Dekker, was suited up and already in the water.

'Is he stuck in the wing? Is he in the other cockpit? Where the hell is he?'

The embarrassing realisation that I'd just wrecked a $10 million boat left me, but was instantly replaced with something far worse: I might just have killed Murray – one of my teammates. This chilling thought then overwhelmed me. It was, without doubt, one of the worst moments in my life.

'Where the fuck is he?'

Five horrific minutes ticked by, and every one of us grappled for an answer. We were trying to unravel what had happened during the incident in the hope we might be able to work out where Murray might have been. Suddenly, a shout rang out:

'We've got him!'

Relief flooded through us all!

It turned out Murray had been in the cockpit of the leeward hull when we flipped and the force of the nosedive had thrown him forwards. He ended up wedged under the deck and so tangled up that he was having trouble extricating himself. Fortunately, he remained above the surface of the water, so survived. Thankfully, somehow no one on board had suffered an injury worth mentioning. This was a miracle considering we had just flipped a 72ft catamaran that had cartwheeled at over 40 knots.

With everyone safe, our next task was to try to save the boat and the wing as quickly as possible, so damage was minimised. Adding urgency to this situation was the fact that the ebb tide was washing us out of the bay towards the Pacific Ocean at a rapid 6 knots!

Medics checked everyone over and, not surprisingly, some of the guys were in shock. We sent them ashore in rescue boats, plenty of which had arrived on the scene by then. We then devised what we thought would be the best way to get the boat upright.

'I am going to climb up the net, attach the ropes, throw them to the chase boats, climb down, stand on the hull and then we'll try to flip the boat back over using the chase boats, just like we did when we

righted the AC 45s on the Cup World Series circuit. I'll then jump on board and keep it head-to-wind while you guys come alongside in the chase boat.'

It all sounded quite logical but, in reality, it wasn't.

I leapt on board and managed to grab hold of the Kevlar netting that I was to climb, but I soon realised that the squares in the net that I thought would be footholds were much too small – they measured just 5 x 5cm (2 x 2in). So, the only way I could then climb the net was by using my arms and fingers, all the time taking the thick tow line with me. It must have been a combination of adrenalin and anger that made this ascent possible because I am pretty sure I would struggle to do it today.

It was really tough going in the rugged conditions, but it wasn't until I looked up when I was 12m (40ft) in the air that I realised the situation was going from bad to worse: we were already drifting under the Golden Gate Bridge. I was close enough to see the engineering brilliance that had gone into the structure, but what grabbed my attention more than anything was the hundreds of people peering over the edge of the bridge watching our ordeal unfold and the TV helicopters in the sky filming the chaos. By this time, our predicament had all the makings of high drama as the Coast Guard had sent one of its frigates to stand by us. I was already thinking the worst: our boat might soon be listed as the latest statistic among San Francisco Bay shipwrecks. Meanwhile, we continued to drift out to sea in washing machine-like conditions…

The good news was that I had managed to get one of the lines secured before throwing it down to a chase boat. My direction to the chase-boat drivers – Ian 'Fresh' Burns, Pete Balash and Rev Minihane – was thus to start towing the boat towards Sausalito on the northern side of the bay.

My next challenge was to get across to the other hull and attach the line there, but as I went it became obvious that things were not going according to plan. The tension on the tow line was causing the cat to go from a headstand position to lying on its side. All we could do right then was hope that the wing didn't break. The guys driving the chase boat went to full throttle in a bid to hold the boat with the sterns in the air, but it just wouldn't cooperate. Part of the problem was that the hulls and wing were filling with water

In hindsight, I have to say that we shouldn't have wasted all that time trying to bring the boat back upright. We should simply have immediately towed it over to Sausalito. Once there, we would have been in calm water, where we could have regrouped and got the job done.

But by this point that opportunity was long gone; we were heading for the wide blue Pacific Ocean in the grasp of a fast-flowing current. However, there was a more immediate danger to contend with. There is a place near the entrance to San Francisco Bay called the Potato Patch – a shallow area that got its name because when you look at it from the bridge the breaking waves make it look like a field of potatoes. If we drifted there, it would be the end of our boat. Right then, we were being washed towards it.

'Fuck, we can't let the boat get into Potato Patch.'

Before we knew it the current had carried the boat straight into it, and the moment it got there, the pounding waves began to devour it. First, the 40m (131ft) wing mast started collapsing like an accordion being pushed together; then huge pieces of carbon fibre, honeycombed aluminium and other structural material imploded with a sickening sound. All we could do was watch the massacre, which was taking place 8 miles offshore, while waiting for the current to turn and the wind to calm down.

Seven hours later – around 10.30pm – a large towboat came out to help us salvage what was left of our boat. Very little of the wing mast remained but at least the platform – the hulls and crossbeams – was intact, so we towed that back to the city, albeit upside down.

Finally, we could all relax a bit but, even so, I realised that some of the guys who had stayed with us into the night were in shock. I was sure this had been caused by two things: the drama of the boat capsizing, coupled with a fear that this would be the end of Oracle's participation in that America's Cup.

At 1am, 10 hours after capsizing, we reached our home base at Pier 80. What had been, just hours earlier, the world's most technologically advanced high-performance sailboat was now at the end of the tow rope behind us looking like a pathetic pile of rubbish – clear evidence that when Mother Nature wants to teach you a lesson, she will always win.

We set about pumping a huge amount of water out of the hulls – cubic metres of it – which made us comprehend it was a miracle that the whole thing hadn't broken up and sunk out there. By then, however, everyone needed to rest, so we left the boat there for the night.

At 3am I drove the 8 kilometres (5 miles) up to my townhouse in the Marina District next to the Golden Gate Bridge, where Jenn and the boys were sleeping. I climbed into bed but quickly realised that there was no way I would be able to sleep. My mind was spinning with all the dumb decisions I had made that day. For example, I knew that where we flipped was known to have the strongest current in all of San Francisco Bay, so why were we there? What had I been thinking? I had put us in the worst possible place even if it hadn't been windy. Why hadn't we discussed the current in our planning meetings, or considered the fact that if we had a breakdown, the current was going to propel us offshore and into danger?

While money is important in an America's Cup campaign, time is more valuable, because the date of the first race doesn't move – the time is finite. So there I was tossing and turning, asking myself how much time this incident would cost the team.

The next morning, not long after I arrived at the base, Larry called. Obviously I was expecting to hear from him, and from the moment I heard his voice, I put my hand up:

'I'm sorry. I was responsible. I take full responsibility.'

'That's not why I called. I know what you guys are doing is tough. Nobody has ever done it before; the America's Cup is not meant to be easy. But I think you guys can come up with a new plan. I still think you can win.'

I was dumbfounded – I didn't know what to say. A couple of seconds of silence followed before Larry spoke again.

'Jimmy, champions and champion teams always come back from adversity and tough situations. In my mind I have no doubt you will get the job done. You guys will come up with a new plan, and you'll figure it out how to win.'

I had arrived at the base carrying a massive burden of guilt towards the team, feeling sorry for myself and depressed, with good reason. I had just capsized and virtually destroyed a $10 million boat. It was probably one of the biggest fuck-ups in the 161-year-long history of the America's Cup – and most of the sailing world already knew about it. Alongside that, it was definitely the biggest fuck-up in the 33-year history of Jimmy Spithill. But Larry's phone call felt like a lightning bolt going through me; it snapped me out of my despondency. He made me realise that wallowing in my own misery wouldn't achieve anything. His words are still crystal clear in my mind. I will never forget that conversation with Larry.

I am sure Larry has gone through a few similar moments in his life to get to where he is today. A self-made man who was adopted at a young age, his attitude is 'OK. It's done. Now what?'

My mind then returned to another element of the conversation we had had that morning:

'We've got to learn the lessons from this ... but what are you going to do, Jimmy? Are you going to sit back and use this as an excuse as to why we are going to lose the America's Cup, or are you going to figure out a new plan whereby you'll grow stronger as a person and the team will get stronger with you?'

Within minutes of that conversation, we had convened a meeting of the boatbuilders, designers, engineers and some of the sailors to work on a new scheme. In a short time we were in the process of turning a disaster into a positive. We didn't just want to repair the boat, we wanted to take this opportunity to improve the concept. Instead of letting the capsize destroy the campaign, it would become the catalyst for building a better Cup defender.

This would be a big test for the entire team. Normally we back each other up no matter what happens, but never had we had to deal with such an extreme challenge. This incident was so large that it had the potential to break a team, so the big question was, could we deal with it? Could the team survive or would we be torn apart by a witch-hunt? But if it was to be a witch-hunt, there was already a culprit: I was to blame. It was unquestionably my fault. In the space of 30 seconds I had trashed what the guys had spent 10 months creating.

Strong growth usually comes from being able to deal with a mistake or a monster fuck-up. When I think of all the stupid things I did when I was younger, I am reminded of the sign on the wall in the boxing gym: 'Defeat is nothing but education.'

If you can be candid and open-minded, keep your ego in a box, and absorb the lessons that come from any trying episode, you cannot help but become a better person. And, if you can do that as a team, your combined strength can be so astounding that you soon find yourselves on the road to success. To function as a team is the ultimate challenge because working together is never easy. The biggest challenge when creating a team is to have people not talk about what they are good at, but to admit to their weaknesses and strive to get better.

Such an attitude emerged from the moment we committed to a rebuild. The shore team working on the boat established rotating shifts that went around the clock. Meanwhile, the designers began modifying the forward sections of the hulls, making them more buoyant so there was more stability when bearing away, and the boat was more efficient when it came to foiling. Other specialists set about improving the shape of our foils so they were less aggressive, as well as developing a control system to adjust the trim angle of the foils, as you would the sails and wing.

I was immersed in the action every day, visiting every section of the team to see how they were progressing. I never failed to visit the builders' shed where the boys in their hazmat suits and masks were grinding and shaping pieces of carbon fibre. This was a terrible work environment, which is why they were completely covered, looking as if they were going into a nuclear reactor. Still, all the time this was going on, I was half expecting someone in the 100 people we had working as part of the team to unload on me – give me a verbal blast, saying 'What were you thinking?' I would not have blamed them for doing that, but not a single team member ever said anything about the incident. It was all about the new opportunities that had arisen as a result.

'We'll get you a better boat.'

'You'll learn from this. The team will be stronger. We'll win.'

This attitude only confirmed what a great team we had. All I could say to myself was, 'If this is how they react as a consequence of the worst imaginable situation – wow!' I felt that a team couldn't pull together any better than this one. This was the sort of group you would want with you if you were in the trenches. It is something I will never forget about this campaign. No one threw in the towel. From that day on, if ever I needed motivation, I would think back to this period.

I don't want to say we were actually lucky capsizing and destroying a brand-new boat, but there were considerable benefits that arose from it. It forced us to make hard decisions. The crash made us question our boat and our campaign in general. It is all about how people perform when everything is on the line.

One of my challenges was to stay match fit during the four months it took to rebuild the boat. To do this, in between all the design and planning meetings we were having at the base, I pushed hard in the gym with my teammates. Still, it was a tough wait for me, thinking about the next sail, and at times I felt haunted by the 'what ifs', like what if we were to capsize again? Then we would really be in trouble.

Four months after capsizing, I was singing the praises of the entire team. The boat was on schedule and ready to go again. How did I feel? Not as worried as I thought I would be. Like everyone else who has been in a similar situation, you just have to get back on that horse and ride it. Even so, we did set limits so that we adopted a more conservative approach to our sailing in the early stages of our trials.

In May 2013, three months after we returned to the water, we were reminded of how lucky we had been. We were out training on the bay with *Artemis*, the Swedish-owned America's Cup team, and waiting for them near Alcatraz. It was a windy day, and they were between us and the bridge. We watched them start to do a bear away, the same manoeuvre we had screwed up seven months earlier. Suddenly, there were gasps filling the air on our boat. *Artemis* flew off her foils and toppled into an even more violent nosedive than the one we had experienced.

'No-no-no-no! Fuck!'

The hull structure failed but, worse still, the wing hit the water so hard that it broke instantly and this caused the boat to flip over and fall on top of everyone. It was the worst possible scenario in a capsize.

I immediately radioed our chase boats and told them to get over there as fast as possible. Fortunately, our safety diver, Jan, was aboard one of our boats so he went into the water the moment the boat got there. It was soon realised that one crewman, English sailor Andrew 'Bart' Simpson, had not been accounted for.

Ten minutes later, Jan located him underwater, trapped under debris. Andrew had suffered a head trauma and was not breathing. He was rushed ashore by a chase boat where an ambulance was waiting and was transported to hospital, but he could not be revived.

The news of this tragedy was radioed back to us, and we all just sat there in stunned silence. While our thoughts were obviously with Andrew, our minds also went back to our capsize and how lucky we had been.

This level of high risk was new to the America's Cup. You can get similar elements of danger in offshore sailing, but just as is the case with mountain climbing, the participants accept the risk as being part of the adventure.

Understandably, there was a belief among some sailors in the America's Cup arena that the contest had become too dangerous. In fact, a couple of the *Artemis* crew walked away for good. Personally, I never thought the risk was too big. I just knew the America's Cup was where I wanted to be and what I wanted to do. That remains my belief to this day.

An independent safety panel was set up following this tragedy and they came up with recommendations that included specifications on helmets, harnesses, the need to carry knives and oxygen tanks at all times, and the requirement that teams openly share engineering knowledge so that we could create a safer environment for the sailors and learn as a group.

Rolling with the Punches

I have often wondered whether the guys running our sport's governing bodies are really in touch with the sport.

I have deliberately stayed away from the different federations throughout my career because they offered me so little. When I was younger, the Australian Yachting Federation (as it was then) was only geared towards selected Olympic classes, but going the Olympic path was never an option to me for one reason – the cost. The sailboat classes chosen by the international body for the Olympics, even the sailing dinghies, were very expensive boats to buy and maintain. On top of that, the campaign costs – including international travel – were exorbitant. I certainly couldn't afford it, and nor could my parents, so I put the Olympics off my agenda at a very young age.

Apart from the money side of things, I never liked the way the organisation was set up. If you were aiming for the Olympics then it seemed they would control your programme, while if you had goals other than the Olympics, the amount of support you could expect was next to zero. So, if you happened to be a young, determined, penniless redhead from Elvina Bay dreaming of the America's Cup, you had no option but to find another way to fund that dream.

Joey, Bull, Andy and I started by organising raffles in sailing clubs and by approaching local businesses for small donations. It was tough going – like scratching in the dirt looking for a speck of gold dust. However, there was one sponsor to whom I will always be grateful – Uncle Ron. In late 1994, when I was 15 years old, he became my first substantial sponsor when he gave me $2,000 so I could buy a new set of sails for the little Flying 11-class dinghy I was racing. More than that, he was an inspiration for me: he had worked his way up from the bottom rung of the ladder to become the vice-president of the big telecommunications company Alcatel.

At this time the sport's governing body in Australia still didn't seem to see the value of putting any resources – human or financial – into match racing. But oddly enough, if I ever happened to have a particularly good year on the Match Racing Circuit, or later in the America's Cup arena, they would happily award me a trophy and lay on the accolades as if I were one of their own. It was an honour, of course, but it always felt a bit strange ... they didn't mind hanging a medal around my neck so the organisation could bask in the media limelight, yet they had never done much towards getting me to where I was in sailing.

Another thing that puzzled me when it came to the federation was how they made their selections for major events. I remember all too well when my sister, Katie, and her crew ended up being one of the teams trying for Olympic selection. Katie had won grade 1 events; a second girl had won the World Championship, while the third contender had never won an event of any significance in match racing. Regardless of this, the federation didn't stage any type of selection event for the three contenders. Instead, they simply decided to select the girl who had not won any major regatta. I don't get that.

I am certain most of the people in these organisations are doing their best. I know there are some really great people in the ranks, but when looking from the outside in, I suspect that there is a degree of internal fighting and political gamesmanship going on.

At times I feel the same with regard to some juries' interpretation of the rules and subsequent judgements, and never were the grounds for my concerns greater than during the lead-up to the 2013 America's Cup.

It all started not long after we completed and won the World Series: in fact the World Series back then was a fleet racing and match racing title at each stop. We had won both the match and the fleet racing event at two events – we had done the 'double' twice, a feat no one had ever achieved. Following the end of the World Series it was decided all the teams would gift their AC45 catamarans used in that series to Red Bull for their Youth America's Cup event. It was a nice gesture that made sense since these boats were going to become redundant because the 72-footers were going to be used for the America's Cup that year.

When the time came to hand over the boats, a team of guys dismantled them so they could be stored. During the reassembly process it was discovered that the kingpost – a structural post that supports the rig – on the two Oracle boats was heavier than those on all the other boats.

Our General Manager, Grant Simmer, told me that lead pellets had been found in the mast kingposts of our World Series boats. I was astounded at this. It was not something I believed anyone on the team would have done. I smelled a rat.

As the Cup defender you are always a target. Everyone is out to beat you or see you beaten. My initial reaction now seems slightly embarrassing, but at the time I was certain that no one on the team would cheat like that and that we were being set up. Adding fuel to this belief was the fact that putting lead pellets inside the kingposts was not a difficult task.

There were suggestions that whoever put the lead there must have thought that the weight would give our boats a winning speed advantage. But tests revealed there was no speed advantage of any significance to be enjoyed by putting the lead where it was found. We are talking about a mere 900g (2lb) increase in weight for a boat that weighed 1,290–1,320kg (2,840–2,910lb) … we're talking 0.0687 per cent of the total weight of the boat! That small amount of weight – or more – could easily have been added in a perfectly legal way with paint or decals if we had wanted. But the lead made us illegal: it was against the rules. While we didn't have any idea when or how this might have happened, we immediately accepted that our boats didn't comply with the rules, so we put our hands up, gave back all the trophies we had won and launched an internal investigation.

Before anyone screams out 'Oracle cheated!', remember two things: first, this 900g (2lb) did nothing to improve the boat's performance or change the overall weight of the boat. We confirmed that by running a Velocity Prediction Program (VPP) and applied all tools needed to simulate what these pellets would do for our speed in a perfect situation. Ironically, the simulations showed that it made us something like 0.000001 knot … slower! To put this into perspective, that weight located in the kingpost was the equivalent of five crew members moving 10cm (4in) forwards. That's something we do all the time out on the water; we are forever moving around the boat to trim it the way we want for maximum speed.

Second, I repeat that these 45ft boats (AC45) had nothing to do with the 72ft boats (AC72) used in the America's Cup final that year. Aside from all this – I don't need to cheat to win. The whole reason I am attracted to sport is that you get a fair go and an even shot. To this day it makes me feel sick that someone could have done this. I could think of no reason for putting the lead in there, apart from it being against the rules, thus making our boats illegal.

I have often been asked how something like this could happen without my knowledge. The answer is simple: when we are on the water all the responsibility is on me, like when we capsized the 72 or if we win or lose. But I can't be in total control when the boat is in the shed being worked on, or is being transported somewhere on a ship. This action slipped through a crack in the organisation – it wasn't legal – but its impact on our performance was the equivalent of a mere drop of water going into a bucketful … there was an infinitesimal change.

However, the America's Cup jury was straight on to us and they convened an inquiry. The jury decided that our wing trimmer, Dirk de Ridder, knew about the lead being in the kingposts, so they decided to ban him. I couldn't believe it. I was as angry as I was dumbfounded! There it was, three days before the start of the America's Cup match, and the jury decided one of our key sailors – the same guy who trimmed the wing on *Dogzilla* and with whom I'd won my first America's Cup match – would not be aboard for our Cup defence. For us, this was like having an arm amputated. Imagine the uproar if Serena Williams were forced by officials to change her doubles partner the day before the Wimbledon finals, or Jason Day were made to change his caddy on the eve of the British Open. That was what had just happened to us. The synergy between the skipper and the wing trimmer on these boats is unique; there is no shortcut and it comes from working together as a team for years.

Dirk lodged an appeal, and the penalty was eventually reduced, but not before his reputation had taken a severe battering, and after the America's Cup was well and truly over.

But there was more to come from the jury...

Another of our sailors, Matt Mitchell, received a suspension for the first four races of the Cup match.

Then it was announced that the Oracle syndicate would be fined US$250, 000!

By this time I was asking myself: where are these guys coming from? What is going on? It didn't add up when you consider the offence compared with the magnitude of the penalty, and especially when it had no effect on the outcome of the America's Cup.

And that wasn't the end of it! Worse was to come.

We were out on the bay training on the 72 while these announcements were being made to the media – but it was the jury's crushing final declaration that caused Grant Simmer to immediately jump on to a chase boat and come out to us to break the news.

'Jimmy, we have to start the Cup match on minus two! They have taken two wins off us as an additional penalty.'

'Well, they should have taken eight, because they aren't gonna stop us. They can take as many as they want, but we're gonna come back from this.'

The jury had gifted the New Zealanders the equivalent of a 25m head start in a 100m sprint.

As the chase boat headed back to shore, we trimmed the sails on the 72 and continued our training on San Francisco Bay, more determined than ever to retain the America's Cup.

Winning the Unwinnable

My Uncle Ron and his wife, Trish, were planning to be in San Francisco for the start of our defence of the America's Cup in September 2013. However, while travelling from Australia he was delayed unexpectedly by a business commitment in Paris. By the time he was able to leave and head our way, things were looking extremely bad for our team; we were on the verge of losing the Cup, so he did the logical thing and called Dad, who was with Mum in San Francisco to support us.

'Hi, Arthur: Trish and I are ready to leave. We can catch a flight from Paris to San Francisco tomorrow, but knowing what's happened I have to ask – should we still come? What do you reckon?'

'Well, Ron, if they lose the race tomorrow they will be presenting the trophy to the New Zealanders before you get here.'

'What would you do – head for San Francisco or head home?'

'You've got to be a realist here, Ron. We are talking about you spending four grand on airfares to get here and see the Kiwis driving off with the trophy.'

'It doesn't look terribly good, does it?'

Uncle Ron's decision was to fly back to Australia.

So, there you have it: neither my father nor my first ever sponsor in sailing, Uncle Ron, thought *Oracle* could win the Cup. The score at that time was 8–1 in favour of the Kiwis, and the first to nine would be the winner.

I don't blame them for not coming; the writing was on the wall in big letters. But I never was one for graffiti or defeat. As silly as it might sound, I was still confident we could turn things around and keep the Cup.

It was because of the incomprehensible penalty the America's Cup jury had imposed on us for the rules violation over the lead in the AC45s' kingposts that we were in this situation. We had to start the competition at minus two points and leave some of our best sailors on shore, which necessitated a major restructure of the crew on the eve of the Cup match. But while we had been dealt a seriously bad set of cards, the only thing we could do was play the rest of the game to the best of our ability. Still, I couldn't stop wondering why the jury had hammered us so severely via the penalty.

So, at 8–1 down, I had a brief yet serious chat with myself: 'OK, we've had some bad luck. All we can do now is get on with it. Stop complaining and deal with the reality.'

As I went into the press conference the media, and especially the Kiwi media, were relentless in attacking our team. After fighting off the non-stop questioning about the team and whether I should be on the boat, I thought back to some advice from Syd Fischer and replied: 'You can be a rooster one day and a feather duster the next.'

I reminded myself that after everything that had happened, coming second in this America's Cup would be like coming second in boxing, and there was no way the team would be giving up and waving a white flag.

I had no option but to put all this to one side so it would not influence my thinking when it came to my own analysis of why we had performed so poorly in the first half of the match. The brutal fact was that *Team New Zealand* was sailing upwind much faster than us, and I needed to know why.

This led to us deciding that the sailing team and our technical experts would conduct an in-depth assessment of the performance of both boats to discover where the differences were to be found.

The Kiwi skipper, Dean Barker, his entire team, and all 4.5 million New Zealanders back home must have thought the Auld

Mug was theirs. However, I sensed this was a situation I could use to put unexpected pressure on the Kiwi team: they had everything to lose at that point and we had everything to gain.

While we had struggled to win a race and the Kiwis got closer to winning the prize, the media – in particular the Kiwi media – wanted to ask me at each post-race press conference how I would feel if we lost. So, at the conference on 12 September, after the Kiwis had scored their eighth win, I had my reply:

'I think the question is: imagine if these guys lost from here? What an upset that would be. I mean, they've almost got it in the bag, so that's my motivation. You know, that would be one hell of a story; that would be one hell of a comeback and that's the kind of thing that I'd like to be part of. I've been involved in some big fight-backs, some big challenges, and faced a lot of adversity, and that's the kind of thing I'd love to be involved in. So, I know I speak on behalf of all the team … that's our motivation going into the rest of this series. We feel that we've got just as much chance to win this and we're going to do everything we can.'

I don't think such a thought had ever previously entered their minds, but now it had. This was a fight to the end, and *Oracle* was still in it.

* * *

Some days earlier, when the Kiwis had won three races while we had won just one, bringing our score to -1 (because of the two-point penalty), we called for a postponement of racing so we could make some changes. One of these involved our tactician, John Kostecki. There are different stories floating around regarding this decision … Kostecki wanted to go; Larry wanted him to go; some guys disliked him. But the fact is that Larry, Russell, Kostecki, our coach Philippe and I all reached the same conclusion at much the same time: JK had made some mistakes and lost his confidence. The fact is that being a tactician when you have a slower boat leads you to take risks, and unfortunately for JK at that stage we had a significantly slower boat upwind.

Consequently, the decision was made … our support skipper, Ben Ainslie, would replace him. But, when I sat down with Ben and asked him to join us as part of the racing crew, he was far from convinced he should take on the role, so much so that he went to Philippe and asked for advice. Philippe convinced Ben that he would be awesome at the job.

Somehow Ben was ready to hear this. During the previous six months he had been racing against us as our reserve skipper. Now, though, here was his chance to really bring something to the team.

Philippe certainly deserves full credit for helping Ben make the decision to join us on the race boat; he was confident Ben would be a great asset in the role of tactician. Even so, crews in this league of sailing often include fiercely competitive guys with big egos: it's all part of the mix and we accept that. However, the great challenge is to get everyone in such a highly talented squad to work as one towards a common goal. That's when the magic happens, and this is when we see Philippe at his best.

So, after four races – three of which we had lost – we had a new tactician on board, but our problem was far from solved because Ben had never previously raced with me in that role, which meant we needed to develop an understanding of each other in a very short time. Also weighing on my mind was the realisation that never before in America's Cup history had such a dramatic change in such a dire situation proved successful for any team. But there was a positive side to all this … the sailing team was ready to make it work.

The change really put Ben to the test; he had to learn how to use equipment that was new to him and master sailing techniques that needed to be applied. However, he and I were ready to deal with these challenges because there was already a strong belief between the two of us that we could make it work.

Fortunately, the positives started flowing from the outset. The first notable difference that came with having Ben on board was that there was a lot more communication between the guys. In particular, our strategist, Tom Slingsby, was now able to get more involved feeding information to Ben and me.

However, there was a lot more to this fight-back than what was happening on the water. I could also sense a never-say-die attitude building among those on shore. Mark 'Tugboat' Turner grew up in New Zealand and has been building boats all his life, including all the boats for Larry and Oracle Team USA. The times I've needed Tugboat and the shore/build team to avert a mistake or when a change is needed last minute are too many to recall. If you were ever in a battle and needed something done, he would be someone you would want there with you. He and his team would work all night if they had to – and trust me, they did. So, to show the sailors' appreciation, I would walk around the compound every night after we came ashore, talking to all of the shore crew, thanking them for their efforts and reassuring them that we could still win. What I found most motivating was that the spirit and self-belief they exhibited matched that of the sailors during a race. They weren't giving up even though the Kiwis had us by the throat.

While we had made a dramatic change to the crew, we knew more needed to be done to the boat if we were to improve our speed. That led to a group of us, including members of the design and sailing team, getting together to explore new ideas. Interestingly, many of the changes we subsequently made were based on instinct more than research, and they all proved successful.

One of many changes we made to improve the speed of the boat – apart from removing the bowsprit – was to change our thinking towards how we trimmed the wing to the wind angle. This made a big difference to our performance, but because we were pushing the boat a lot harder, the loads exerted on the wing went beyond their designed structural limits, and that was scary. Regardless, we had to push our luck and hope it all stayed in one piece.

This dilemma was never more evident than when I asked Scott Ferguson, our wing designer, what increasing the camber of the wing to make it more powerful would mean for the structure:

'I don't know, Jimmy, I'm worried it will be too much and it could break.'

'Scotty, frankly we don't have a choice. We need to try something so we have to go with it.'

Any day that racing was not scheduled we were out on the bay training while, much to our surprise, the Kiwi team kept their boat on shore. It was as if they felt they did not need to go out and train. But every day we went out we found small changes that could be made to make the boat more competitive. This meant when we craned *USA 17* out of the water each evening the shore crew would set about making the modifications we recommended.

The biggest change in making the boat go faster was how we were sailing it, and a lot of the credit needs to go to the youngest member of our crew, Kyle Langford, who days before the start of the America's Cup was thrown into the deep end, having to replace Dirk de Ridder as wing trimmer. Trimming the wing on an AC72 is like holding the accelerator in your hand: you essentially control how fast the boat goes. Over the years we had sailed together, Dirk and I had built a strong relationship on the boat, while Kyle and I only had a few days' preparation. But fortunately he had a lot of talent as well as a great work ethic and attitude, and we started to get in sync with each other pretty fast. Being wing trimmer, as well as the youngest on board, he had no shortage of advice from on and off the water – and I was really impressed with how he handled it all. I'd first met Kyle when he joined us on the RC44 circuit back during the 2010 campaign. He'd instantly fitted in and brought a bit of fun to the team. We were fortunate enough to win a lot of races that year, as well as the World Championship.

Once back on the racecourse our new-found speed, particularly when sailing upwind, put added pressure on the Kiwis as well as on our boat – so much so that when the score was at 6–0 in their favour they had a near-capsize, which came as a result of human error on their part. It was a costly mistake: we went on to win quite easily. This result meant that having then won two races, our score remained at zero because of the two-point penalty we carried into the event. But the good news was from that moment on any other wins became positives for us.

Bit by bit, I felt the confidence growing within our whole team; the momentum was building and things were starting to go our way. We had no doubt that the near-capsize was the first sign of cracks appearing. With each subsequent race we were able to apply more pressure to them and this led to more and more opportunities.

Regardless, they were still able to march on to a score of 8–1, a situation that, for us, was like standing in front of a firing squad: they were just one race away from winning the America's Cup.

The pressure was then really on us: we needed to win eight races straight if we were to defend the prize.

Race Day 9: the Kiwis did their best to outmanoeuvre us at the start but we managed to counter their move and led from start to finish, our winning margin being 31 seconds. This was the day when they, and everyone else, began to realise that *Oracle* was then a very different boat, especially when sailing upwind. At one stage we topped 32 knots. Another contributing factor was our ability to execute a new high-speed tacking technique that made us even more competitive. We were so efficient that we made gains on just about every tack during the race. The roar of jubilation from the thousands of American supporters lining San Francisco's dock-front, along with those on spectator boats around the course, gave our confidence a much-needed boost. The believers were back and we needed them.

The score was then 8–2.

On the eve of the next race my cell phone started buzzing. I had the ringtone turned off because I was in a meeting in which we were analysing everything we needed to do to make the boat even faster, but on seeing Aaron's name flashing on the screen, I excused myself and answered the call. Aaron had been with us in San Francisco for the opening days, but had then had to return to Auckland.

'Hey, Jimmy, it's me. I heard on the radio that you're on to something and you're back in the game. So I called the office and cancelled my meetings. I'm coming back. I'm at the airport now, catching the next flight to San Francisco. I don't want to miss this – and I'm bringing your brother and cousin with me.'

'Good news, mate. See you soon.'

'Cool, see you soon.'

Race Day 10: The next race was sailed in light winds of around 8 knots, the softest we would see in the regatta. We won the start but *New Zealand* fared better than us in the conditions and extended their lead on every leg. On the fourth and final leg to the finish, they were more than 1,000m ahead of us and the Cup looked to be going their way. However, even though things seemed really grim for us, there was still a chance we would stay alive, but that chance was out of our hands ... it was with the weather. Should the wind fade it was possible the Kiwis wouldn't reach the finish line within the 40-minute time limit – and that's what happened. The race was cancelled. I don't believe there is luck in sailing, but I have to say the weather was on our side that day. The re-sail of the race was run the same day, and we won it comfortably. The margin was 1 minute and 24 seconds, the Kiwis' largest defeat so far. Now the score was 8–3 ... and we were on the march.

Race Day 11: Racing was cancelled because of fickle winds, but that gave us the opportunity to get out and practise. Even though we were under a lot of pressure, and we were in the middle of the regatta, we kept looking to make any improvement, large or small, radical or basic ... anything that would improve our speed. It was either that or lose. That's why we trained and trained and trained until we were finally mastering foiling upwind – which the Kiwis couldn't do at all. Once we could sail on the foils upwind, we were off like a startled gazelle. However, it was a balance and there was considerable and vigorous debate; some of the guys wanted to go to smaller foils, but this would have prevented us from sailing on foils upwind. So it was really a case of trusting instinct when making the final call.

Upwind foiling would prove a game changer. Tom Slingsby had suggested it months before the Cup and both teams had been trying to achieve it leading into the racing. But it was so difficult to get it right without throwing away a heap of VMG (velocity made good – a situation whereby you might be able to sail a longer distance upwind in a shorter time because of your increased speed). Fortunately, we were starting to figure it out, but it took a heap of coordination between our wing trimmer, Kyle, and me. At the same time, the winch grinders had to be going full throttle on the handles for the entire upwind leg, so we had the power needed to continually adjust the trim on the sail. Because of this demand we had to change the way we used the winches so we could guarantee maximum power. Instead of having four guys operating two coffee-grinder pedestals, which had been the norm, we then had eight guys continuously operating all four pedestals. This in itself was a huge change in our sailing technique, but we knew it meant that when the wind permitted, we could foil upwind.

Whenever possible, we trained at wind angles we could expect on the racecourse. The actual Cup course was unique in that it had been designed to accommodate high-speed catamarans and ensure the boats and crew were tested on all points of sailing. The total length of the course was approximately 10 nautical miles (19km) and it generally took 25 minutes to complete. It consisted of five legs, starting with a short reach across the wind, then a downwind leg, an upwind leg and another downwind. The final leg was a short reach to the finish line on the waterfront where spectators watched from grandstands. This course was always an intense test for crews but that generated great excitement for everyone, including the international television audience.

At the end of this practice day, I went home feeling the best I had in weeks. For the first time since the campaign started, I knew we had the Kiwis' measure, and our guys finally believed we had the boat that could do the job. From the beginning, I always had faith that we could come back but after that day's practice session, I really knew it.

Race Day 12: It was 22 September, and that took the America's Cup series into its third week, equalling the previous longest regatta in the Cup's history, the 31st America's Cup, which was staged in Auckland. We had an unexpected visitor approaching the course before racing commenced – a whale – but fortunately it decided to cruise away and not become part of the action. On the first scheduled race of the day, we led from start to finish, but on a few occasions had to apply our best tactics to make sure the Kiwis were held at bay. Our winning margin was 23 seconds, and that, much to our delight, took the score to 8–4. Still, we needed five more consecutive wins to retain the Cup.

In the second race of the day, *Team New Zealand* were to windward, but we had the favoured leeward position and this allowed us to reach the first mark with a slight advantage. The downwind leg that followed was one of our best: by the time we rounded the next mark we led by a minute. We covered *New Zealand*'s every move upwind and lost some distance but still won the day … our best day so far.

Race Day 13: There was only one race staged this day, and by the time it was over, the Kiwis knew the enemy had them in their sights. As soon as the start signal was made, we were able to get *Oracle* on to her foils and in no time we had charged into the lead amid a cloud of spray. The Kiwis could then only look at our sterns for the rest of the race, which ended with us scoring a 33-second win. With our fifth win in a row, the score was 8–6, and from that moment the Kiwis knew they were on the back foot. It was becoming apparent to us that they were feeling the pressure as they kept making an increasing number of small yet time-consuming mistakes. I showed no mercy at the press conference either, telling the media that we were constantly changing the boat to make it faster, statements that put further pressure on the Kiwis and had them guessing.

Race Day 14: From the outset we showed the New Zealanders no mercy. We went after them and we managed to nail them with two pre-start penalties. That proved to be a great advantage for us. We led by 18 seconds at the reach mark, and went on to win by 27 seconds. That result took us to 8–7, which meant that the media was like a wolf pack in a feeding frenzy:

'You really should have won by now – how does it feel?'

'You could be holding the Cup right now. How do you feel about that?'

Of course, they were referring to the two-point penalty we had to carry into the event, but to me this was evidence of sports journalism at its worst. There was no way we could be holding up the Cup at that time ... we hadn't won yet. I struggle to understand why so many journalists place so much emphasis on the hypothetical instead of reality. I had only one answer for them:

'We're not going to stop – we're going to keep going all the way to the end. We really want this. You can sense it on board.'

In the second race of the day, the Kiwis got the jump on us at the start and scorched away to the reach mark at just under 50 knots. They maintained their lead to the downwind mark but soon after heading upwind, they gifted us the lead by making a poor tack. We capitalised on this opportunity by getting our boat up on to her foils and went on to win by 54 seconds. The score was now 8–all: the scene was set for one of the all-time great races in the 162-year history of the Auld Mug.

There was now only one race that mattered in this America's Cup and, for just the third time ever, it was winner takes all.

Race Day 15: Apart from capsizing, we couldn't have had a worse lead-in to this crucial race. While we were tuning the boat on the bay prior to the start, there was a loud bang from the wing's middle section. The noise was so loud that we thought it was a major structural failure, and we feared the worst. One of the control arms had cracked. The rigging team led by Andrew Henderson and Jeff Causey rushed to us and came on board. Jeff was hauled up in a harness to a point about 10m (33ft) above the boat. He located the problem and shouted to us that it was repairable, but there was still a chance it might not last the race. He set about doing a makeshift repair, stuffing epoxy glue into the cracks while our shore boss, Mark 'Tugboat' Turner, and his guys were cutting up pieces of carbon-fibre plate and hoisting them up to him.

While all this was happening, the crew and I were using the time to analyse the weather forecast and plan our tactics for the race. The media were right on to us: might we not be able to race at all? Will the fitting fail again during the race? They had their headlines.

All the while and off in the distance, Emirates Team New Zealand were practising on the start line and doing laps around the course. Still, there was no guarantee we would be able to race. While the noise of angle grinders carving up carbon fibre continued, we could only live in hope and plan tactics. It was not the ideal preparation for one of the most important races in your life but it was all we could do. At one stage, Ben and I looked at each other and laughed. We realised that while we had the weight of the nation on our shoulders, we had to retain a sense of humour. If we didn't, the pressure of the moment would cause us to crack.

After some 40 minutes Jeff rappelled down.

'Give it as much time as possible before you start pushing the boat so the glue can cure.'

'No worries, mate.'

As soon as the shore crew were off the boat, we trimmed the wing and went to full throttle. There was no holding back; we couldn't wait any longer as we were about to enter for the start.

This final race was no walk in the park for either team. The Kiwis were a tough bunch. On the first leg of three, we had a big nosedive that gave them a lead, and had me very concerned about Jeff's repair, which, without doubt, had just been tested to the limit – but then conditions became perfect for high-speed sailing. Both boats were foiling at 40 knots with the Kiwis showing the way. However, we were far from being beaten – we were close enough to them on the final upwind leg to get ourselves into a position where we could pass them. Here again, it was evident that our hours and hours spent practising foiling upwind was about to deliver its dividend – all our hard work was paying off. Once we were in the lead, I knew that they would have to climb over us if they were going to beat us. We rounded the bottom mark and scorched towards the finish line, crossing it 44 seconds ahead of the Kiwis.

The atmosphere among our supporters and the spectators was euphoric, but for the crew and our gallant and tireless shore team, it felt as though the war had just ended. We struggled to realise what we had achieved, but we knew we were the winners.

Interestingly, the adrenalin that had kept us going for so long suddenly evaporated, but soon this was replaced by total joy for everyone. Personally, it was as though a huge weight had been lifted from my shoulders.

Larry jumped on to the boat and began hugging all of us. At the same time I was being mauled by the rest of the crew and our support team on the chase boats. The noise from the crowd and spectator fleet was almost deafening.

Comeback Consequences

'Bugger!'

This now legendary one-word tweet from the New Zealand Prime Minister, John Key, said it all.

New Zealand was a nation in mourning. Shock and disbelief had swept across the small and proud country after we came from being 8–1 down and retained the America's Cup for the USA.

So, while the Kiwis were cancelling victory celebrations, Oracle Team USA was launched into the stratosphere. First up there was the victory party in front of thousands of people at the America's Cup village on San Francisco's waterfront – a memorable time at which the boys and I had yet another chance to just about drown Larry in champagne. Then it turned into a champagne fight among the rest of us. However, my most vivid memory of this moment was seeing my mother up on the stage, planting a congratulatory kiss on Larry's cheek after I introduced her to him amid the chaos. What is it with women and billionaires?

The next few days were like being part of a full-on but weird movie, where no one was quite sure what the next twist in the plot would be.

We started out by heading to a private concert organised by Oracle on Angel Island featuring Maroon 5 and Black Eyed Peas. Next it was a Red Bull-sponsored basketball tournament at Alcatraz where the star was one of the NBA greats, Blake Griffin, of the Los Angeles Clippers. The added attraction for us was that, for the first time, we were actually on the island around which we had sailed countless times when training for the Cup match. While the prison is now abandoned, there is still a cold and uncomfortable aura about it – so much so that every one of us was glad not to be staying a few nights.

The next major event on our agenda came when we were invited by the owner of the San Francisco Giants baseball team, Larry Baer, to join him in the dugout at the famous AT&T Park before a big game. It was thrilling for us to meet so many of baseball's living legends, but much to our surprise, they were just as eager to meet us following our win. Every one of them offered us congratulations and wanted to shake our hands. Before the game started, an amazing number of kids in the crowd wanted autographs from anyone who was wearing Oracle gear... including Aaron, my brother, a cousin and a few other mates. At first they tried to explain that they weren't part of the team, but nobody was listening to that, so for the first time in their lives they were signing autographs and being recognised as heroes. All I can say here is that if you were one of the kids who got your cap or your baseball signed with names you don't recognise from the boat, you have not been conned by an imposter. They may not technically be part of Oracle Team USA but they were definitely part of our extended family.

Our comeback win made headlines across America and much of the world, and as a result I had to do a seemingly endless number of interviews on national TV, including late shows, and also for print media. It was an arduous agenda – unlike anything I'd ever done before – but while I sometimes wished during that period that I wasn't the skipper of the boat and could wind down, I had to accept it was part of my job. Needless to say, everyone in the team was exhausted after such an intense effort over so many months. Many, including myself, actually became ill when it was all over simply because we were so fatigued. All I really wanted to do was to go home and rest and spend time with my family and friends, but I had to hang in there; I had an obligation because our sport and the America's Cup was finally getting high-profile recognition with the public. I was representing Oracle Team USA and every one of its members, so I didn't want to let anyone down. Russell kept reminding me 'You've got to do this', but I don't think either of us realised how many weeks the punishing schedule would continue, during which I would be required to fly the length and breadth of the country. No matter where I went, our victory was heralded as the greatest comeback – ever. It was something that had never been experienced in America, and probably not in any other country either.

Before long, invitations were arriving from overseas. This meant that Jenn and I travelled to Kuala Lumpur in Malaysia to attend a major sporting dinner because our win had been nominated as one of the greatest sporting comebacks of the year. Many in the audience were surprised that Rafael Nadal won and not Oracle Team USA, but I accepted that with ease, particularly since he has always been one of my heroes. Another highlight of the evening for us was to meet some of the real legends of sport, including All Blacks Sean Fitzpatrick and Dan Carter, cricket legends Steve Waugh and Jacques Kallis and legendary skater Tony Hawk. The list of names went on and on, but what made the night even more satisfying for me was to realise how many of these legends had watched us racing in San Francisco.

There was to be one other significant accolade coming my way that year: I was named World Sailor of the Year.

In New Zealand only two things really matter: the America's Cup and the All Blacks rugby team. The Cup match in San Francisco was front-page news every day; the entire country was sitting on the edge of their collective chairs, with their thumbs on the champagne corks, ready to let them go. Cue our comeback: the country plunged into the depths of disappointment.

I have to admit I sympathised with them because I have a deep respect for New Zealand and its people. My association with the America's Cup began there. It's also where I met Jenn and later married her, on the South Island, and we have a lot of friends there. In general, the Kiwis were always positive and very supportive of what I was doing – I always remember how the grannies came to our shore base with cakes in the *Young Australia* days. But our winning in San Francisco caused a lot of people to not exactly like me: I was Public Enemy Number 1.

Of course I had been a bit cocky and arrogant at the press conferences during the Cup match, but that was all part of the game. I wanted to unsettle the Kiwis, especially since I believed they might be vulnerable. I remember one day when Joey came up to me after a media conference and said: 'Mate, the Kiwis aren't enjoying your comments in there,' which to me meant I should keep it going and even turn up the heat a notch.

In reality, most of it was tongue in cheek. Kiwis and Aussies have this constant rivalry going on. For example, the Kiwis wear shirts with a slogan reading 'I barrack for New Zealand and any team playing Australia'. That's how it is and I don't have a problem with that.

Unfortunately, though, some Kiwis were so incensed by our comeback and subsequent victory that it triggered something I found extremely disturbing. I was trolled on the internet before and after we won. I wouldn't have cared if it had been aimed only at me, as was the case with the bullies at school, but when this guy using an alias started writing on Facebook the address of our houses in San Francisco and New Zealand, together with photos, and going on to make terrible comments about my family, it had gone too far: it was abusive and menacing. This was not freedom of speech – it was a really nasty vendetta aimed at my family and me.

When it got to this level, I immediately contacted Aaron as both his father and his brother are among New Zealand's top private investigators, his father being a former cop and detective, one of the true tough old school legends. It turned out that they had already spotted this weirdo online after he overstepped the boundaries and entered the illegal realm, threatening the safety of innocent individuals.

They didn't muck around. Within a few hours they were able to pinpoint the perpetrator: he was a Kiwi living in London. However, instead of sending the police to his front door, the investigators contacted a rather tall, somewhat imposing Bulgarian gentleman they knew who subsequently paid him a visit. Within an hour we had a photo of the offender, a signed statement from him and a guarantee that everything he had written would be removed immediately. I was surprised and impressed by how easy it was for experts to track down this lowlife. This really makes me wonder why there are so few cases of legal action against trolls and why so many investigations are abandoned owing to lack of evidence. I am greatly concerned when I think of kids, in particular, who are being targeted by these cowards who hide in the online world.

After all that positive and negative attention it was a relief to return to home turf in Australia and, even though there had been no Australian participation in the America's Cup for some time, I still fielded many interview requests from the media. When all that was done, I was able to take a much-needed break without any interruptions, primarily because Jimmy Spithill is not a household name there. It felt good to be able to walk down the street without being recognised.

All I wanted to do while in Australia was to take it easy and hang out with the kids and friends, so I was not too concerned about the fact that I wouldn't be sailing in the annual Sydney to Hobart race that starts on Boxing Day each year. This meant I could relax in front of the TV watching the start of the race, then an hour later switch over to watching the cricket – the legendary Boxing Day test match. Seeing the start of the Hobart race had me wishing, just slightly, that I was there, but I knew that being at home and in such a relaxed environment allowed my body and my head to take a break. Also, I accepted that had I decided to go to Hobart Jenn would have killed me!

While in Sydney I also attended a yachting award ceremony and, when there, caught up with Syd Fischer for the first time in years. In classic Syd fashion, he made an oblique reference to my winning the America's Cup, after a not-so-subtle reminder of a comment he made when I worked for him, one that has stuck with me ever since:

'Remember that you can be a rooster one day, and a feather duster the next.'

'Ha-ha, yep, I know, Syd, I'll never forget that.'

'Anyway, well done with everything. You owe me one – I really taught you a lesson back then.'

I managed to smile as I didn't really know how to reply. In hindsight he did teach me a lesson. It was his way of saying: 'Be careful when you sign something … don't be naive. This is the real world and if you are not careful, people will take advantage of you.'

NINETEEN

Bermuda

About a year after Oracle Team USA successfully defended the America's Cup it was decided that San Francisco would not be considered as a venue for the next match, America's Cup 35, scheduled for mid-2017. When it came time for the decision on the venue to be made, there were three contenders: San Diego, Chicago and Bermuda. To the surprise of many, in December 2014 it was announced that AC35 would be staged in Bermuda.

As the Cup defender, our team immediately began making plans for establishing a base there, and set about developing a defence programme.

Along with the core of the sailing team, I moved to Bermuda in early 2015 and from that moment on, we went into a rigorous training schedule that was aimed at making sure we were as fit as humanly possible and perfectly prepared for the Cup match. At the same time, every part of our planning for the defence was gathering momentum.

Jenn and I found a nice waterfront house at Warwick that suited our lifestyle, so that became home. Most mornings, around 6 o'clock, while Jenn and our boys were still sleeping, I would leave home, cross the road and walk down six steps to our little stone dock where my white 18ft motor boat was moored. I would jump on board, turn the ignition key, cast off and take in the fenders, then head for our base 6 kilometres (3.7 miles) to the north.

For me, the Bermuda America's Cup set-up was the best to date: there was no better way to start the day than to go to work by water while watching the sun come up. As my little boat sped across the Great Sound towards the old Naval Dockyards where our base was located, it left a wake that looked like a jet's vapour trail. I took time to enjoy nature at its best, especially the sunrise and the beautiful surroundings.

I distinctly remember one morning reflecting back to my childhood on Pittwater, in Sydney, and realising I had come full circle ... from being a little boy dreaming of the America's Cup while heading to school on a ferry chugging out of Elvina Bay, to this moment when I was zooming to work by boat for my second America's Cup defence. However, as pleasurable as these solitary journeys were, my mind wasn't always on the positives.

I've read books and listened to successful athletes and high-profile people who are adamant that they live their lives with no regrets. I understand and respect that viewpoint, but it doesn't apply to me: looking back, there are things I would have done differently.

Like most people, I have made mistakes – big and small – so I can say that living with regrets is a double-edged sword. On the one hand, they force me to try harder and push myself forwards, yet they also haunt me because I carry a burden of guilt.

I am usually thinking of Paulie whenever this guilt surfaces.

My fundamental rule has always been: 'Don't let your mates down.' This was drilled into me by my grandfathers and coaches, and then reinforced by my participation in team sport and my fascination with Navy SEALs and special forces in the military.

Kiwi Paul Wallbank was a great mate, as loyal as they come. He had a sporting background – golf – and ultimately ended up in boxing, where he trained some of New Zealand's top fighters and was one of the best guys on the pads in the sport. Some of the Kiwi greats such as Kevin Barry, David Tua and Daniel Codling were associated with Paulie.

We first met in 2002 during the *Oneworld* campaign in Auckland, when Paulie was running a small boxing gym in a car park next to the Les Mills health club. I did a few sessions with him, and from that moment we just clicked. We both loved boxing and had similar stories relating to how the discipline had put us back on track in life. As it turned out, the Oracle team hired Paulie as a trainer for the 32nd America's Cup in Valencia, but while I was there with Prada's *Luna Rossa*, we never caught up because our days were so long and busy.

Cue the 33rd America's Cup: I joined Oracle, and who was standing there on the first day I walked into the gym – Paulie!

'Hey, Jimmy Spithill – you wanna do some pads?'

'Hell yeah, brother!'

We trained almost every day for the next couple of years – pads, weights, running, sparring – you name it. He would travel with us around the world to numerous regattas … the RC44 circuit, TP52 championships and the Extreme Sailing Series. Paulie's attitude was always so positive: he would do any job asked of him and train everyone in our team. There wasn't anyone who didn't love Paulie – from Sir Russell Coutts to the girls in the office and the guys sweeping the floors.

Paulie and I were like two peas in a pod when it came to sports; we would play golf, tennis and relentless matches of ping-pong – anything competitive. And, if there was a boxing World Title fight coming up we would be as excited as kids on Christmas Day. Even so, it wasn't always easy to find somewhere we could watch the bout. Often, when we were away at a regatta in Europe or America and there was a big fight happening, we had to wander through the backstreets of strange towns in the hope we could find a bar that would show the fight on TV. I don't think we ever missed one, and sometimes our enthusiasm for the fight led to the bar owners keeping their premises open after hours just so we could watch it to the end.

The fact was if Paulie was your mate you had nothing to worry about. He would always be there to help: the sort of guy who would jump in front of a bus for you.

As I am sure everyone who knows me well is aware, I have an addictive, obsessive personality, so when I get into an America's Cup campaign it is the only thing on my mind. I think more about winning and defeating my competitors than I do about my family and friends. It's an unfortunate truth. The fact is I am no angel, so much so that I often wonder how Jenn puts up with me.

Without going into too much detail, I knew that Paulie was going through a rough period in his life, but instead of making sure he was OK by talking to him, I just assumed that everything would be all right.

I was wrong.

I lost sight of Paulie's problems because I was so absorbed in my own life and its demands.

The dreadful news came in a phone call from our team's general manager, Stephen Barclay:

'Jimmy, it's Stephen. Paulie is dead.'

'What!? Can't be – I was with him yesterday.'

'I am sorry, mate. We all are. Let's head down to The Rocks, that bar we used to drink at with Paulie…'

Stephen kept talking but I didn't hear a word. In a heartbeat my mind went into a state of shock and confusion; I was dumbfounded. I felt like I'd been king-hit by Mike Tyson. I was emotionally knocked out while desperately wishing I could turn back time.

I will never forgive myself for letting down Paulie – it's probably my greatest regret in life. To this day I continually think about him. But, fortunately, I have managed to draw a positive from this tragedy: I use his memory as an inspiration when I need to be stronger and more understanding of others.

When we crossed the finish line and won the America's Cup with *Dogzilla* in Valencia, Paulie was the first person I thought of. Then, during the comeback in San Francisco, I was always thinking of him and felt his presence. I didn't want to let anyone down, but in particular, him. Maybe that's how I come to find the strength I need when things aren't looking good.

Paulie, I'm sorry mate and I miss you, brother. See you on the other side.

* * *

Each day it took me around 10 minutes to get to the Oracle base from home. It was located within Her Majesty's Dockyard, Bermuda – a cluster of historic buildings that was the principal base for the Royal Navy in the Western Atlantic in the period between the American War of Independence and the Cold War. While we occupied some of those buildings, a mix of tents and shipping containers were also part of our set-up. It sounds simple, but it was like a well-oiled five-star army camp with a fantastic canteen next to the boatsheds. The working day always started in the gym, which was located inside a 200-year-old building. We had every facility and piece of equipment we needed, including a boxing ring. The sessions were led by our head trainer, Craig 'Oscar' Macfarlane, with assistance from Paulie's successor, Brent Humphreys, to whom in fact Paulie was a mentor. Brent and I became great mates – our friendship is now as strong as the one I enjoyed with Paulie. His nickname is 'The Honey Badger', and he's been in my corner for the last two Cup matches. Brent really was a catalyst when it came to bringing the team together, training sailors, the shore team, designers and some of the guys' partners and wives. Everyone loves The Honey Badger.

There were about 80 people working at our team base, and every one of them wore team gear. It was a uniform that reminded us why we were there and that we were united as one. Those employees ensured we had every base covered – sailors, trainers, chefs, designers, engineers, boatbuilders, riggers, PR people … the list goes on.

Just as was the case in San Francisco, we were determined to have the best team possible.

To achieve this, we insisted on having an open planning environment. A lot of good ideas come from young heads and people new to the team – they often bring a fresh level of thinking. Of course you need a blend of experience in there as well, but very rarely does a breakout new idea come from people who have been associated with multiple Cup campaigns. Often the latest members of the team will say nine silly things, then suddenly deliver a gem of an idea that no one had previously considered – a brilliant thought that might enable us to take the next step.

The key is creating an environment where people are not afraid to ask a question. In some cases this may even lead to looking again at an idea that was previously dismissed.

I always tried to take a back seat in this environment. I felt it was important to show restraint so I could encourage other people's thought processes without influencing their ideas or way of thinking. That's my leadership style – subtle encouragement. It's something I learned from Larry and Russell and my Uncle Ron – all great men. It's not about paying lip service; you must really listen and show genuine interest. I have one pet hate: anyone who talks over the top of someone or doesn't let that person finish what they were saying.

* * *

When the wind conditions were right for sailing, our shore crew would have our catamaran, *USA 17*, dangling from the crane on the dock just before lunch, ready for launch. On the days we decided to sail, it would take an hour from when that decision was made to when we left the dock and headed out on to the Great Sound, where the fun began.

The advent of hydrofoiling brought unprecedented levels of excitement to sailing events across the world, none more so than the America's Cup. However, because it was a totally new dimension in the sport, the learning curve for sailors was very steep.

The AC50 catamarans, which were developed specially for the America's Cup in Bermuda, were far more technologically advanced than the 72-footers we saw in San Francisco, and their design concept certainly differed in many ways from those of their predecessors. For a start, in an effort to reduce costs, the AC50s were basically a one-design wing-sail catamaran, where the hulls and many of the other major features of the design were identical. They measured 49.2ft (15m) overall, were 27.8ft (8.47m) wide, had a maximum weight of 2,432kg (5,362lb) and a six-man crew. The ultra-lightweight hulls were constructed from a carbon-fibre sandwich with a honeycomb core – very much space-age technology.

It was the efficiency of the 100sq m (1,076sq ft) wing sail, and the hydrofoils, that contributed most to the boats' speed. The two foils were retractable L-shaped daggerboards located amidships in each hull, and the two rudders, or elevators, were the shape of an inverted 'T'. Once we refined our sailing techniques we were able to have the AC50s up on the foils and flying in just 6 knots of wind. At maximum speed they could sail between three and four times faster than the strength of the wind – sometimes near 30 knots upwind and 50 knots downwind. It was all about the boats' design and our sailing technique breaking the drag barrier. This was achieved by having the most efficient foils in the water and minimum windage above the water.

There is nothing that can be compared to the feeling you experience when the hulls lift clear of the water and you begin foiling. It is as if you are sailing on a cushion of air, as at that stage you have only one of the hydrofoils and the bottom of the two rudders in contact with the water. The big challenge is managing the interaction of wind and water – two elements that have completely different densities. There is no such thing as a steady state when you are foiling: you are always working your hardest to keep the boat flying as the wind strength and angle changes.

As a helmsman, you are the equivalent of a jet-fighter pilot and a racing-car driver moulded into one: constantly adjusting the buttons and twist grips on the steering wheel to change the trim of the boat by just a few degrees so you can have the hulls at optimum height above the water. The wing trimmer is constantly moving the wing, through a combination of sheet control and hydraulic actuators adjusting camber and twist profile throughout the entire span. Simultaneously, the rest of the crew are grinding non-stop on their pedestals trying to give you the power and oil pressure to keep all these controls – and more – functional. If you can't keep up or you run out of oil, you will crash.

When it comes to being on the water, there are many old-world, die-hard sailors who are adamant that catamaran racing is not tactical or exciting. Those guys are plain reactionary – they just don't get it because they don't want to. I have been a monohull and multihull sailor all my sailing life, and I can assure them that multihull sailing is just as hard and tactical as any other form of the sport, but the big plus is you travel much faster, and athletically are pushed harder, and that is seriously exciting. Simply put, you are better rewarded for your hard work.

* * *

For me, the best thing to come to the sport beyond the America's Cup was that, during this same period, we were able to pioneer long-distance hydrofoil sailing offshore in large catamarans.

In November 2016, Red Bull sponsored our 46ft Gunboat catamaran, *Team Falcon*, for a 662-nautical-mile high-speed run from New York to Bermuda. However, while this was great fun, for me as skipper it wasn't quite the experience I had in mind.

After waiting a couple of days for a hurricane to clear, we set sail, hydrofoiling at high speed past the Statue of Liberty and out into the Atlantic. Everything went according to plan all the way out to the Gulf Stream – we were on record-breaking pace for the passage – but then, when we were 100 nautical miles east of the US coast, Mother Nature changed her mind and slammed shut the favourable weather window she had earlier opened for us.

Within hours, we were trapped in a rapidly developing storm. In no time the wind had increased in strength to 45 knots but, worse still, the waves had grown to be 8m- (26ft-) high monsters that were towering above the boat and, at times, breaking over us. We had no option but to lower all sail and run downwind with the storm under bare poles. The waves were so powerful that we were constantly under threat of nosediving and going upside down. Fortunately, I had a highly experienced crew with me so we applied every ounce of seamanship we possessed so we could stay as safe as humanly possible. Among this team of seven, Shannon Falcone and Rome Kirby were two guys I had done a lot of sailing with and both had competed in the Volvo Ocean Race. While this drama was unfolding, I was constantly getting flashbacks to the horrid storm we had survived aboard *Ragamuffin* in the 1998 Sydney–Hobart race.

We were in a lot of trouble for 36 hours, during which we remained in survival mode. I have to admit we were lucky to get through unscathed, and it reminded me yet again of the awesome power Mother Nature can unleash when she chooses. Eventually, we got into Bermuda 66 hours after departing New York. Luckily I was able to radio some of my teammates, led by shore boss Andrew Henderson, Rev and Ryan Barrango, to come out in one of our big chase boats to help us through the reef. The fact that they came out in those conditions, in the middle of the night, is something I won't forget. Without their assistance we may not have made it in.

If there was a plus to all this, we learned a lot about how to handle the boat in such extreme conditions. It was also a great test of seamanship for everyone on board. Added to the challenge was that I was still on 12-hourly intravenous antibiotics. I had convinced my surgeon, Rob Bray, that we could train Rome to administer these to me – so we had the needles, plumbing and drug packs. But I will never forget, in the middle of the night, Rome and me trying to put a needle into my vein as, outside in the storm, Shannon and our photographer were holding the IV pack up in the air, trying to get gravity to do its work as we launched down and into the troughs of waves. I guess it's not meant to be easy…

Regardless of the conditions we had to survive, this offshore adventure confirmed that in the not-too-distant future we will see large hydrofoiling multihulls making an assault on the non-stop round-the-world speed record. This is currently held by French yachtsman Francis Joyon, who in 2017 amazed the sailing world by completing a circumnavigation, which started and finished in France, in the astonishing time of 40 days 23 hours 30 minutes 30 seconds, claiming the Jules Verne Trophy. I expect that in years to come a similar-sized hydrofoiling multihull will better that time by a considerable margin.

Close to Losing a Wing

'You know, Jimmy, quite often athletes think they have a problem in some part of their body but it proves to be a mental thing. So I think it is possible that the problem you have with your elbow might actually be in your mind.'

'Wow. But it's really painful under load.'

'Well the MRI shows no tear or damage.'

So there I was, sitting in a doctor's surgery in the summer of 2016, totally perplexed. Was the pain in my left elbow real or was it in my head?

This was not the first time my tendons had troubled me and it was not the first time I'd been given a bad diagnosis. It was due to me overdoing it at training and steering the boat constantly for hours on end. Being on the wheel the entire day – while the boat applies its G forces – means I'm applying a high-tension grip on the wheel for all that time. Also, I'm using my fingers to simply hold on. Little wonder, then, that my tendons started to give me grief.

The fact is that I had been carrying this pain with me for some time, thinking it would magically go away and that I would train through it. As it was persisting and since I was not able to get a definitive answer as to its origin or cure, I decided to seek a second opinion and to seek it from the best.

I sent a note to Dr Robert S Bray Jr, whom I knew through Red Bull. He is a legend among athletes, who call him 'Doctor Fix-it' – a spine surgeon recognised globally for his neurological surgery skills and for being a pioneer of minimally invasive surgery. His practice has a reputation for hiring only the best of the best and consequently he can fix anything from spines to heads, shoulders, knees and toes. He had already fixed my other arm following the Cup in San Francisco, after I had been through the final six weeks of the campaign with a torn tendon known as 'golfer's elbow' (I wish it had been from golf...).

When I spoke to him, Dr Bray had one message for me: *Get on the next plane to Los Angeles and come and see me.*

On arrival there, I jumped into a cab and went straight to his clinic, located in Marina del Rey. He immediately sent me to get an MRI done, and after 20 minutes of hissing, humming and clicking sounds, I went back into his office to look at the results.

He scanned them for about a minute in silence, narrowing his eyes and really focusing on the images before delivering his verdict:

'Sure enough, you have torn it.'

He then honed in on the damaged area that the MRI was revealing. He pointed to a part of my elbow where I could clearly see a split surrounded by what he explained was inflamed tissue.

'Look, Jimmy. There is the tear...'

'Shit, I knew something wasn't right!'

I had already had some cortisone shots in Bermuda, but those didn't help. However, as I was still within the limits of what a body can take, Dr Bray gave me another cortisone injection.

Ah, the relief that came from simply getting it to the right spot! For the first time in months I was able to use all my senses without being slightly numbed by an ever-present pain. This shot was so on target it got me, pain-free, to the Portsmouth Louis Vuitton America's Cup World Series in July, where we were able to climb up the points table to second spot overall – just one point off the lead.

But you can only put lipstick on a pig for so long. Cortisone provides temporary relief; it is not a long-term solution. Surgery was inevitable if the problem was going to be fixed, and sailing in Portsmouth certainly ensured that was going to be necessary. We were in the middle of one of the races on the Saturday when I felt the tendon go. I knew immediately I had torn it off the bone as my elbow got really hot. As it wasn't my first rodeo when it came to tearing tendons, there was no doubt in my mind as to what had just happened. There was nothing else I could do but think, 'Oh well, I've done it now. I'll be seeing Rob on Monday.'

At that stage we were close to the Brits on points, heading into Super Sunday.

Although on that Sunday we were the top performing boat, the Brits had just done enough on the Saturday to win the event by one point, and after I had been introduced to HRH Prince William and HRH The Duchess of Cambridge at the trophy presentation, I hightailed it to the airport in London and boarded a transatlantic flight back to Dr Bray.

I have had a few surgeries during my life when I felt like a robot going in for a hardware update, but I wasn't at all worried now that I was seeing Dr Bray, who lived up to his reputation.

But Rob gave me strict instructions: I needed to take it easy and let the arm recover. Nothing but time and rest would heal this. 'Of course, mate,' I told him, 'no worries…'

I was looking forward to going back to the daily routine that I loved with the lads, but it was too much too soon, and I became the perfect example of the damage that can result from impatience: I overdid it, and although initially my arm showed no sign of pain or discomfort, it became seriously infected. I remember while we were training on the water, the chase boat came alongside with Philippe, our coach. 'Are you OK, mate?' he asked. I didn't say anything but showed him my elbow, which was starting to look like a balloon, with some nasty fluid coming out of the incision. 'We should to go back in, Jimmy – that doesn't look good.' It turned out that I had caught a form of *Pseudomonas* bacterium and it was enjoying a feeding frenzy in my arm – so much so that I was told I might lose the limb.

Dr Bray, who is not one to exaggerate, told me that had I waited another day or two before coming back to his clinic, I would have walked out with one arm having been amputated, as did so many of the war heroes I love reading about. Alternatively, I would have had chronic arthritis from then on, which is another legacy of this nasty bacterium.

Unfortunately, this bug was very aggressive and persistent so the infection kept returning. What had caused it was no doubt rushing back and getting the wound wet. So from September to November I was commuting between Los Angeles and Bermuda for more surgery, while taking heavy doses of intravenous antibiotics which were pretty strong and knocked me around a bit.

This led to me missing the Toulon AC World Series event in France and having to watch from the sidelines. Tactician Tom Slingsby moved back to steer, and Sam Newton replaced him in his position. But unfortunately with the shuffling around and the lack of time to train in that combination, we got our worst result of that season while the Brits moved into the overall lead.

During that time, all I could do to keep in shape was a bit of running. I awoke that Sunday to find my arm leaking that same nasty substance I had seen before. I rang Rob immediately – although it was 2am in Los Angeles – and he picked up on the second ring.

'Hey, Jimmy – what's up?'

'Hi, Rob – I think I may have re-infected my elbow.'

I showed it to Rob on FaceTime and got the same answer he had given me before:

'Get on the plane now. We'll end this once and for all.'

So after an emergency flight out of Toulon to Paris, thanks to my mates at Red Bull, I boarded a US-bound plane and Rob's team picked me up from LAX. I went straight into surgery on that Sunday afternoon. Rob had called his team in on their day off to fix me!

The flip side was that Dr Bray very kindly invited me to stay with him and his family for the few weeks I was in Los Angeles recovering after surgery. I don't think he trusted me any more to take it easy and probably figured this would be the best way to keep an eye on me. I don't know how many doctors would invite their patients to live with them, especially when they have a young baby. But over the course of my stay we became really good mates because we found out we had a lot of similar interests. He's an ex-military guy who loves sailing, and has had a lot of interesting experiences in his life. We were fortunate to have him join our team and help a number of teammates during the campaign.

I think you really meet only a handful of 'real' mates in a lifetime – guys who would jump in the fire for you and go beyond the call of duty at the drop of a hat. Rob Bray is one of them and I'd happily do the same for him without even thinking about it. He is a guy you would want on your team when heading into battle on the sporting field. He has that never-say-die attitude and is relentless in his pursuit. He doesn't stop until he has won – or, in his case, fixed a problem.

So, after being on heavy intravenous antibiotics morning and night for eight weeks and having multiple surgeries, I had my last injection in November 2016, on the eve of the final World Series event in Japan. Midway through the competition the Brits sealed the overall title and secured the two bonus points. It was now between Team New Zealand and us for runner-up and the last remaining bonus point, which would be applied to the Qualifiers in Bermuda. We ended up in our own match race at the back with them and outsailed them to walk away with the point. The Kiwis left with third place and no points.

TWENTY-ONE

The Match

Coming into the business end of the America's Cup, I knew we were going to have the fight of our lives with whoever ended up getting through the Challenger Series to face us in the Cup Match.

We had had an indication of what to expect during the Louis Vuitton-sponsored AC World Series in the lead-up to 2017. This had been sailed in identical one-design AC45 foiling catamarans with a crew of five, and concluded in Japan at the end of 2016. The format worked like this: overall first and second places on the AC World Series would be awarded bonus points that they would carry to the Qualifiers – first place receiving two points, and second place getting one point. Each point would be translated into the equivalent of one win in the Qualifiers.

Land Rover BAR won, we were second, Emirates Team New Zealand were third, Artemis Racing were fourth, SoftBank Team Japan were fifth and Groupama Team France rounded out the rear. This meant that the Brits would start the Qualifiers on two points and we'd start on one.

Each team launched their one and only AC50 during early 2017. Following a sea-trial period, informal practice racing in the AC50s was scheduled in Bermuda in the run-up to the Qualifiers.

We were already guaranteed a spot in the America's Cup Match because we had won the previous America's Cup in San Francisco. However, as the Defender, we couldn't compete in the Challenger Playoff semis and finals.

The protocol, or set of rules, put in place for this America's Cup meant that we would, however, be competing in the round robins, with the incentive of a bonus point for the America's Cup match – the equivalent of a win – being up for grabs. This meant that if we as the Defender won the double round-robin Qualifiers, we would start the match at 0, and the challenger at –1. If one of the challengers won the Qualifiers and went through the semis and finals to face us in the match, they would start on 0 and we would start at –1. This prevented any match fixing or sandbagging from both sides.

Of the five challengers, the top four would go to the semis, while we would then train on our own as we waited for the top team to come through.

Lining up our AC50 for the first time against another team was really exciting; it was the first time as a group, with the exception of ETNZ, that we could all get a read and see how we fared. Initially, it was good news for Artemis, Japan and us – with very similar performances – although Land Rover BAR were struggling for speed and clearly had some work to do.

The French arrived not too long afterwards, and showed signs of launching late since they were having onboard control system issues and were really battling for stability.

The Kiwis were the last to arrive and clearly looked fast on the water. Like us and the Japanese team, ETNZ had opted for extremely unstable and aggressive foils. However, unlike anyone else, their set-up featured four 'cyclors' or cycling sailors – as opposed to the conventional 'coffee-grinder' arm-powered system – to power the systems required to keep these boats sailing on the edge.

Another big difference was that my old mate Glenn Ashby was using a hydraulic system with a 'Game Boy'-style control box to adjust and control the shape of the wing as well as the small jib in front of the wing. This was in contrast to most of the other boats, aboard which the helmsmen had to control the angle of attack or pitch adjustment of the foils using a system located on the wheel.

On our boat, we started out with a series of buttons on the rim of the wheel – similar to the set-up in San Francisco – but this then developed into twist-grip adjustors featuring small steps, much like the system used for changing gears on a mountain bike. The Kiwis, meanwhile, had developed an outfit that enabled Blair Tuke, who was on a bike, to fly the system by looking at a display. This had the major benefit of freeing up Pete, who could consequently get his head up out of the boat to look around rather than being head down focusing on riding the boat at the target ride height – both in a straight line and, more importantly, during manoeuvring and in the starting box.

Despite these Kiwi innovations, it was difficult to pick a favourite heading into the round robins. The pre-racing had been really close between us, Artemis and SoftBank Team Japan, with all three of us trading wins, and although the Brits and French were still struggling for consistency, they were getting faster as time went on. The Kiwis, meanwhile, had only competed in a few pre-races but looked sharp.

As expected, many thought that this was the best racing ever seen in an America's Cup, with constant lead changes, closing speeds at 80-plus knots, upsets and crashes. Amid the excitement, we managed to reach the end of the series, thus setting up a showdown between us and ETNZ for the bonus point for the Match and to decide the winner of the Qualifiers.

As in the previous race, we won the start, inflicting a penalty on ETNZ. We then had a great back-and-forward battle before giving them another penalty at the top mark as we entered the final leg of the course, and went on to take the race as well as the bonus point, and won the Qualifiers.

This was a good confidence boost for the team – it was a high-pressure race with a lot on the line and the team responded. However, I wasn't alone in being concerned about how fast the Kiwis seemed. Even when making mistakes, they always appeared to have the ability to come back and create opportunities if they were behind. In addition, when ahead, they would generally extend away.

Their manoeuvrability was really impressive. Because of the way their inboard systems worked, they could manipulate their boat without any of the crew being required to relocate for set-up. This meant it was impossible for their opponent to know what their next move was going to be. None of the other teams could do that.

Coming in second in the Qualifiers, ETNZ became the top challenger and, not surprisingly, they chose to race against the Brits in the semi-finals, leaving Artemis and Japan to race each other in the other group. The French, who caused a few big upsets, lacked sufficient time in the boat to make the semis and their America's Cup was now over.

The Brits had made some good gains, but not enough to catch the other three teams. This in spite of the fact that the Kiwis had during the build-up suffered a major capsize and then, in a separate race, broken their wing. When it came to it, the Brits were simply no match for ETNZ and they lost 2–5.

On the other side of the draw, Artemis Racing and SoftBank Team Japan had a great battle, but ultimately Artemis proved too strong for Japan – who had exactly the same boat as us – and they took the win 5–3.

The outcomes of these two races set up a Challenger Playoffs final between Artemis Racing and Emirates Team New Zealand, which again would provide a fascinating insight for us.

Artemis won every start but one, but very early on it was clear that ETNZ had made a big jump in performance. They now had the ability to come back and create opportunities – and when they made a pass and got in the lead, they simply sailed away, especially in the light-wind conditions. This meant one thing: boat speed. They were significantly faster.

In a couple of races it looked like they had got their foil selection wrong for the weather, but despite this we were all shocked by just how much range they had in their boards. We knew we would have our hands full after they had dispatched Artemis 5–2, a score that could have easily have been 5–0.

Waking up knowing you are racing in the America's Cup is always an amazing feeling – a mixture of nerves, excitement, energy and adrenalin. It is difficult to put the sensation into words, but it is why everyone in the game, regardless of their role, works so hard in the years preceding that moment. And now, almost four years after we'd won race 19 on 25 September 2013 in San Francisco, we were once more going back into battle for race 1 against the Kiwis.

Looking at the forecast for the opening weekend raised concerns – our weather models were showing wind of just 6–8 knots for the next 10 days. As we'd feared, ETNZ were fast, especially in the light air, and over the first weekend of racing – through a combination of speed and out-sailing us – they quickly won four races to end up ahead 3–0 (they started the competition on –1 as a result of us receiving the bonus point for winning the Qualifiers).

We now had five days before the next racing weekend during which to try to make some serious changes. However, having studied the weather models, it didn't look like the forecast was improving for us because wind speeds were predicted to remain under 8 knots. We really needed 12 knots or more in order to be close in performance.

So, we went about trying to bring our up-range foils down range. Simply put, our light-air foils were thicker and carried more wetted area than those of ETNZ. Our only hope was to bring our smaller high-speed foils down range to match their area, and we did this by increasing span on our foils and eating into our engineering safety margins.

We also went for the most aggressive rudders available, which had just been built by Tugboat and his team. Originally designed for near-drifting conditions if we were in almost no wind, these rudders really made the boat tough to drive, to the point of making it almost un-sailable. It was now very difficult to sail in a straight line, let alone manoeuvre, especially in the starting box, but we knew we had to take a risk. As usual, the team collectively went all in with this philosophy, because we knew that if we didn't make drastic changes our chances of winning were doomed.

Watching the shore, boatbuilding and design engineering teams working 24-hour shifts during that five-day period in order to allow us to sail was really inspiring. Out of all the teams I've been part of, Oracle Team USA consistently came together in tough moments and displayed the never-say-die attitude better than anyone else.

As expected, Saturday brought more light conditions. Despite this, we were able to get our important first race win. However, although we had improved our boat speed, we were really struggling with stability with our current set-up. The fact was, though, that we didn't have a choice – we had no option but to keep pushing and trying to claw our way back into the competition.

Unfortunately for us that was to be our only race win for the series. In race 9, at match point, we came out with the attitude that we could win races *if* we sailed perfectly. We had to minimise any mistakes, since we knew how quick these guys were. So, for only the second time of the match, we were able to get the jump off the start and lead them to Mark 1. However, once more ETNZ was able to pull off a manoeuvre we were not ready for and, without moving any crew, gybed and instantly overtook us having layed into the bottom gate after we'd left our gybe a little too late. The boys fought hard on board, refusing to accept we wouldn't win the race, but for the final time ETNZ crossed the finish line ahead of us to claim the 35th America's Cup.

I was absolutely gutted. It is difficult to describe the feeling after a loss like that but I guess I would use the word 'empty'. No one really talked on board and we sort of withdrew into our own worlds. The entire team had put everything into it, left nothing in the tank, but it still hadn't been enough.

Through better sailing – starting, tactics, boat handling and manoeuvring – and impressive boat speed, the better team had won the America's Cup. The first thing we did after crossing the line was head over to the Kiwis and give them a thumbs up and applaud them. What an impressive campaign they had run – really with no apparent weaknesses.

Following that I went round the boys on the boat and thanked each of them for their efforts. I had asked them before departing the dock to leave everything on the race track today, which they had done, and I was proud of them. We then made our way to the presentation mooring off the Race Village and stadium.

As we arrived ashore Larry was there to shake our hands. He got to me and I apologised for letting him down. Without skipping a beat he responded:

'Jimmy, when you go against the best in the world, you can't expect to win every time. They were just too strong this time. Over the last three America's Cups we've won two of them, that's not a bad result.'

It was typical Larry, to the point and gracious in defeat like a true champion and sportsman.

Having shaken hands with all the Kiwis and thanked Bermuda on the stage, I went into a private hospitality area to wait before my final press conference. The boys then left to head back to the base to see our teammates.

As I was waiting there alone, Russell came in and joined me, bringing with him a couple of cold beers. We then had a really open and honest chat, reflecting on the racing and the campaign. He said to me I couldn't stop now because I had unfinished business, being tied on 14 America's Cup wins with him as a skipper, and I didn't want that hanging over my head. We shared a few laughs and I really appreciate that he stayed with me at that moment.

If it hadn't been for Russell giving me an opportunity back in 2008 I am not sure I would have won two America's Cups. He was someone I had looked up to as a kid, and who had subsequently become a mentor and a mate for me as well as a boss. He is one of the most candid people I know, and he and Larry brought this game into the mainstream and gave so many young kids opportunities to get into the sport and the America's Cup.

This was not the case prior to us winning the Cup in 2010, when there had been no pathway for the next generation into the America's Cup. The typical route then was to hit the Match Racing Circuit, but that in itself didn't guarantee anything. It was both Larry and Russell who pushed to have a Youth America's Cup, which very quickly gathered the support of several partners and became known as the Red Bull Youth America's Cup. Did it work? Well, the guy who'd skippered the winning team during the Red Bull Youth America's Cup in San Francisco had just helmed the Kiwi boat in the main event of AC35, so I'd say so. In addition, several youth team members had been recruited by all of the teams in this latest Cup.

During this last campaign, we also started the Endeavour Program for kids aged 9 to 12 years old. This gave them the option and means to learn sailing when they wouldn't otherwise have necessarily been able to do so. More than 1,550 kids went through the program in Bermuda.

Having been involved in developing both of these programmes, I'd discovered that it was something I'd really enjoyed and I got a lot out of giving back. The mission was to leave the Cup in a better place and I think this was achieved well. I'm still left with the images of kids being given boats, which our boatbuilders had repaired and turned into brand-new boats, as a reward for outstanding training and commitment. This was definitely one of the highlights I will take with me from my time in Bermuda.

To be honest, I don't really remember much of the final press conference. As always, I spoke from the heart and remained candid, not shying away from answering honestly. But really all I wanted to do was get back to the team and thank each and every one of them again for their hard work and support and apologise for letting them down.

Not long after arriving at our base, the sailing team grabbed me and we went into our locker room one last time for a few drinks and to share a few stories. Out of all the campaigns, this was the best group of mates I'd been with – we really had no egos and everyone got along great. Win and lose, we remained a close and tight-knit team to the end without assigning blame.

A few of us thought as a mark of respect we should take our chaseboat over to the Kiwi base and share a beer to congratulate them. So, I rang Glenn Ashby, who picked up straight away.

'Hey mate, we want to come and share a beer with you guys as a mark of respect.'

'Absolutely mate, I will be waiting on the dock for you blokes.'

The sailing team piled into our chaseboat and motored over to the other side of the Kiwi base, where Glenn was waiting.

I remember from my rugby days, after playing a tough game or a final, having won or lost, you would always go into the other team's locker room or have them in yours to share a few beers and laughs. It's one of the things I love about sport – you try and kill each other on the field of play or in a boxing ring, yet moments afterwards have your arm around the shoulder of your opponent, usually having swapped jerseys, enjoying a cold one and reflecting on the battle.

Unfortunately, I hadn't seen this much in the America's Cup and it felt good to share a few beers and laughs with the Kiwis at their base. We stayed for a couple of drinks, but then wanted to leave them with their supporters and families to really savour their moment. We also wanted to get back to ours.

As we walked down their dock and into our chaseboat the Kiwi supporters came down and clapped us off. It was something we all appreciated and that I will remember. They were a class act.

TWENTY-TWO

Now What?

I find it amusing that some of the sailing media are questioning me about my age and if I may be finished now that I'm 38. Personally, I've never judged someone when it comes to age, how they appear or where they come from.

I look instead at the sporting world, in particular MotoGP – arguably a sport that requires the most split-second reactions at speeds of over 350km/h (217mph) on a motorbike – which is still dominated by 38-year-old Italian legend Valentino Rossi. Elsewhere, Tom Brady at 40 is still leading the New England Patriots to Super Bowl titles and Roger Federer at 36 is still winning Wimbledon. I could go on and on.

I've always hired people on the basis of their talent, work ethic and ability to put the team before themselves. But for some reason certain media – and especially some of the sailing media – seem to love getting caught up in immaterial questions, which is likely why they will remain watching from the sidelines.

If I look back on this campaign, when we had the same one-design identical AC45s as we'd had on the AC World Series, we beat the younger guys at their own game. Peter Burling and Nathan Outteridge must rank as the best in the world when it comes to high-performance fleet racing – between them they have dominated the 49er class, which is the pinnacle of Olympic one-design fleet racing, and the foiling Moth class – yet, with the same one-design foiling catamarans, we beat them. Actually, the guy who beat us and won is in his 40s – Sir Ben Ainslie.

Regardless of the fact that we were the Defender, we still won the Qualifiers and the Kiwis were runners-up. I don't think anyone could argue that both teams shouldn't have been in the America's Cup match.

But, again, I use the armchair critics as motivation, just like I did back when I was bullied as a kid and people questioned us at Young Australia.

It's an interesting time following the end of an America's Cup campaign. Win or lose, I find myself reflecting on all the mistakes in order to really try to understand how we got there, what are the lessons we can learn and how we can get stronger. This process goes on for some time, but is a really important one personally and as a group. I still to this day believe more than ever that defeat is nothing but education.

Ultimately we were too conservative in a lot of areas, and as skipper I take full responsibility. At the end of the day, as Larry told me following the AC72 capsize:

'Champions and champion teams always come back.'

You only need to look at ETNZ following their brutal loss in San Francisco in 2013. Clearly, this is a champion team and you can do nothing but have an enormous amount of respect for them to have been able to regroup, keep fighting, get stronger and return to win in Bermuda.

When I look back at my career in this game I've been living the dream:

- Six cup campaigns;
- The most America's Cup race wins as skipper, on par with Sir Russell Coutts;
- Greatest comeback in the history of all sports;
- Won the Cup and defended it.

What an amazing opportunity I've had to be involved in some fantastic teams, getting to meet and learn from the best in the world, and looking forward to getting up every single day trying to be better than I was the day before.

Muhammad Ali won the world title three times, which means he lost it three times too, and he is the greatest boxer in history.

I'd like to be remembered for getting up off the canvas – not for hitting it. I've just come off copping one of the biggest hidings of my life, but I ain't no feather duster.

Not done yet.

THANK-YOUS

There are hundreds of people who deserve thanks, individuals who were part of the teams and my life, who influenced me on this journey. Even if you are not mentioned in the book, thank you.

FAVOURITE WORDS

'*There is no second...*'

The reply to a question from Queen Victoria aboard the Royal Yacht off Cowes, England, in 1851

'*Come on – one more!*'

Paul Wallbank – Auckland, New Zealand

'*The harder you train, the luckier you get.*'

'*Defeat is nothing but education.*'